W9-BML-232

The Religious Situation

The Religious Situation

THE RELIGIOUS SITUATION

by PAUL TILLICH

Translated by H. RICHARD NIEBUHR

LIVING AGE BOOKS

published by MERIDIAN BOOKS *New York* 1956

Paul Tillich

Paul Tillich is a faculty member of the Divinity School of Harvard University. From 1933 to 1954 he was Professor of Philosophical Theology at Union Theological Seminary in New York City. Born in 1886, he was educated in Germany and held university positions there until 1933. Conflict with the rising Nazi regime ended his professorship at Frankfurt-am-Main. Among his books are *The Interpretation of History, The Protestant Era, The Shaking of the Foundations, The Courage to Be; Love, Power, and Justice; The New Being,* and his major work, *Systematic Theology,* on which he has been concentrating for three decades.

Living Age Edition published by Meridian Books, August 1956

First printing, July 1956

Reprinted by special arrangement with Henry Holt and Company, Inc. Copyright 1932 by Henry Holt and Company, Inc.

Library of Congress Catalog Number: 56–9242

Manufactured in the United States of America

Publisher's Note

The publisher is proud to present *The Religious Situation* to the public at a time when Doctor Tillich is recognized as one of the formative minds in American life. *The Religious Situation* was written when he was exerting significant influence on the intellectual and religious life of Germany. During the intervening three decades, Doctor Tillich became a refugee from the political tyranny which arose out of the situation which he had analyzed. Now known throughout the United States as a teacher, writer, and lecturer on issues in contemporary culture, he has nevertheless stated, in *The Religious Situation*, the plight of twentieth-century civilization with striking incisiveness.

The signs of protest against a self-sufficient culture which he describes have not diminished, although their specific historical manifestations are new. The developments of our time have accentuated doubts about the rationality of science and technology. Political and religious forces, their alignments and their hopes, remain astonishingly similar. And Tillich's treatment of the Protestant principle in terms of its power and its fault remains relevant to our religious situation. This is a prophetic book which gives a clue to the history of our time and the ground of cultural renewal.

The Religious Situation was published in the United States before Doctor Tillich came to assume his influential role at Union Theological Seminary. At the time of its publication it was not widely distributed, and has been unavailable for many years.

Doctor Tillich has recently become University Professor at Harvard University, where he continues his work as philosopher and theologian.

Contents

Contents

TRANSLATOR'S PREFACE

Paul Tillich's *Die religiöse Lage der Gegenwart* is one of the most important of the many attempts which were made in modern Germany to achieve the orientation of thought and life in the new world of the twentieth century. It is not a book about the religion of the churches but an effort to interpret the whole contemporary situation from the point of view of one who constantly inquires what fundamental faith is expressed in the forms which civilization takes. Tillich is more interested in the religious values of secularism, of modern movements in art, science, education, and politics than in tracing tendencies within the churches or even in theology. Back of this book is the conviction that modern civilization is not only on trial but that it has been judged and found wanting and that in the struggle for a new world more is at stake than the discovery of new political and economic organizations which will enable the West or humanity, for that matter, to survive a while longer. The book is an earnest and profound attempt to discover where we stand and to ascertain whether there are creative forces at work in the catastrophes of the time.

Briefly, Tillich argues that what we are witnessing and participating in is not the decline of the West but a revolt against the spirit of capitalist society. Capitalist society, however, is not a scheme of economic organization only; it is also a culture with a definitely religious character. Its civilization is based upon faith in the self-sufficiency of the human and finite world; its hope and purpose is the establishment of human control over the world of nature and mind. Natural science, technique and capitalist economy —a trinity of powers which reinforce each other —support and control the civilization. The spirit of human and finite self-sufficiency is expressed in painting, sculpture, education, politics and religion and gives rise everywhere to an attitude of human domination over things in which there is no respect for the given and no true appreciation of human or any other kind of individuality.

The revolt against capitalist civilization has

not been confined to communism. On the contrary, communism in its later phase, since it has lost the prophetic character of its early years, has adopted much of the spirit of capitalism so that the Russian Revolution may be regarded as one of the greatest triumphs of the spirit of capitalist society. The revolt against this spirit became manifest first of all in art. Its precursors were Cezánne, van Gogh and Gauguin. In literature Strindberg and Nietzsche were its earliest prophets. In science Einstein, Planck and Bohr and other founders of the new science of the twentieth century, in philosophy Bergson, Simmel and Husserl, in psychology Freud, in education a multitude of reformers, in morals the youth movement—all are representative of the revolt. Tillich attempts to interpret the significance of these tendencies as protests against the spirit of capitalist society and as prophecies of a new attitude.

The new attitude which is developing in consequence of these revolutions may be described in religious terms, he believes, as an attitude of "belief-ful realism." The term is strange and paradoxical and it is intended to be so. Religion for Tillich is "direction toward the Unconditioned." It is the reference in all life to the ultimate source of meaning and the ultimate ground of being. This ultimate transcends experience and knowledge though it is that to which all experience and knowledge refer. It is apprehended only indirectly through the symbols of the finite world. Nothing temporal, nothing finite, no one object among other objects, or no one value among other values can be designated as the ultimate. It is always transcendent and therefore unknown, yet the reference to it is implicit in life and wherever there is any meaning this reference to an ultimate source of meaning is present. The religious reference may be present in culture, in art, science, politics, education and the economic life, but in these spheres it does not become explicit. It is taken for granted; it is an unacknowledged presupposition. In religion in the narrower sense of that term the reference to the Unconditioned becomes explicit. Since the Unconditioned is forever hidden, transcendent and unknowable, it follows that all religious ideas are symbolical. They are good symbols when they point unambiguously to the transcendent; they become false symbols when they are regarded as possessing an intrinsic meaning or when they claim absolute value for themselves. A belief-ful realism is first of all an attitude in which the reference to the transcendent and eternal source of meaning and ground of being is present. This reference has been absent from capitalist society with its reliance on intra-worldly, intra-temporal sources of meaning, its exaltation of the finite into an absolute.

In the new movements of revolt the reference to the Unconditioned is once more making itself manifest or, at least, the negative conditions for the rise of the religious reference are being created. Where this reference to the ultimate is present there the first term of the paradox, the element of belief, asserts itself. But belief or faith must be mated with a realistic attitude toward things. A belief-ful idealism tends to spiritualize its objects, to regard them no longer as symbols of the ultimate or as deriving their meaning from the Unconditioned but as significant in and of themselves. A belief-ful realism, on the other hand, does not idealize or spiritualize its objects. It is the skeptical, unromantic, unsentimental attitude which accepts the objects in their stark givenness. It sees the world with the sober eyes of the scientist or realistic artist, accepting it at the same time as symbolic of the eternal and unconditioned source of all meaning and ground of all being.

"Belief-ful realism," Tillich writes, "is a total attitude toward reality. It is not a theory of the universe, neither is it a kind of practice but it belongs to a level of life which lies underneath the cleavage between theory and practice. It is

not a particular kind of religion or theology. In
fact it is not any kind of separate, particular
thing. By the connection of *belief-ful* and *realism* the most fundamental of all dualisms is
called into question and if it is justly called into
question it is also overcome. Faith is an attitude
which transcends every conceivable and experienceable reality; realism is an attitude which rejects every transcending of reality, every tran-
scendency and all transcendentalizing. In view
of the antithesis of these attitudes it is natural
that the mind should be inclined to evade the
tension which results from their union. Evasion
is possible in one of two directions, either in the
direction of a beliefless realism or in the direction of idealism. Beliefless realism forbids all
trespassing over the boundaries of experienceable reality. Its noblest form is to be found in
positivism, which needs by no means to be irreligious but can assign religious objects to the
realm of experienceable reality. Pragmatism
proceeds in this fashion, very consistently in
America, less consistently in the empirical theology of Germany. In the case of idealism even
one's feeling for what is linguistically permissi-
ble resists the suggestion that the adjectives *belief-ful* or *beliefless* might be added to that
term. This is due to the fact that idealism transcends experienceable reality and cannot there-

fore be designated as beliefless so that the antithesis disappears. Consequently idealism can
claim, with apparent justification, to be in itself
and immediately belief-ful. But this formulation of the claim contains implicitly the criticism
that is to be made. To say 'in itself and immediately' is to omit just that which faith means
—the transcending of reality, that is an attitude
which cannot be reached on the basis of reality
and which must therefore stand in unconditioned tension with reality. From the point of
view of faith idealism also is a beliefless realism,
from the point of view of realism it is too transcendental or transcendentalized. In this double
attack from faith and realism idealism is destroyed. It is overcome by one side or the other,
historically and systematically, in life and in
thought. Its excellence lies in its effort to reconcile the necessity of abiding in the real with the
necessity of going beyond the real. Its limits and
its tragedy lie in the fact that it transcendental-
izes rather than transcends the real and so is
unable to do justice either to realism or to faith.

"Hence we are led to the surprising result
that faith and realism, just because of the tension which prevails between them, belong together. For in faith the unconditioned tension is
present and no attitude which weakens this tension can be associated with it. Idealism weakens

it, beliefless realism cancels it, belief-ful realism expresses it." [1]

Tillich has been quoted at length on this subject because the concept is central in his thought. The idea is inherently difficult and the difficulty of translating the finer nuances of his expression does not improve the intelligibility of the definition. The reader will do well, however, to think of the realism of art and history rather than of the realism of epistemology in the first place in attempting to understand Tillich's position. The belief-ful realism which he recommends and finds developing in modern movements is the antithesis to a "technical" realism which is interested in reducing things to their general and utilizable terms. This realism seeks to fit things into the scheme of rational concepts and to identify their actuality with those elements in them which can be handled in thought and practice. A belief-ful realism, on the contrary, is willing to concede individuality and uniqueness to things. It sees them as independent of the human mind, as purely given things, which may indeed be analyzed in part for purposes of control, which, however, never reveal the whole secret of their being to generalizing analysis but only to sympathetic intuition. Hence Tillich finds greater religious value in a

[1] *Religiöse Verwirklichung*, Berlin, 1930, pp. 67-68.

still-life by Cezánne or a tree by van Gogh than in a picture of Jesus by Uhde.

Belief-ful realism is closely related to a theory of history in which the decisive importance of the present is emphasized. Tillich, following Troeltsch, Rickert and Dilthey as well as many great historians who concerned themselves with the problem of the meaning of history, is an historical realist who emphasizes the category of individuality in history. He has abandoned the liberal myth of unending progress and it is impossible for him to accept the old orthodox mythology of history. Whatever values these conceptions may have had in the past they are not useful to-day. The myth of progress has been destroyed not only by the realism which the events of the time have taught but also by the realism of historical research, which discovers that the uniqueness and unrepeatability of historical events are quite as significant as the general sociological laws which may be represented in them. The myth of progress, furthermore, expresses that sense of the self-sufficiency of the temporal order which Tillich finds characteristic of the whole capitalist civilization. It does not recognize that all time receives its meaning from its relation to eternity, to the Unconditioned. Orthodox mythology on the other hand finds the meaning of history not in the secular process, even with its reference to the ultimate, but in a super-history or a sacred history which parallels the history of this world. Tillich, rejecting both of these views, turns to the conception of *Kairos* for the adequate symbol with which to express his sense of the meaning of time. "Kairos is fulfilled time, the moment of time which is invaded by eternity. But Kairos is not perfection or completion in time. To act and to wait with the sense of Kairos is to wait upon the invasion of the eternal and to act accordingly, not to wait and act as though the eternal were a fixed quantity which could be introduced into time, as a social structure which represents the end and goal of history, for instance. The eternal is that which invades; it is not something tangible and objective. There are societies which are turned away from the eternal, which rest content in time and finitude, and there are other societies which are turned toward the eternal and which express in their forms the judgment that they have experienced as proceeding from the eternal. But there are no societies which possess the eternal." [2] Every period of time is related to the eternal but not every period is aware of this relation. Consciousness of the relation arises only when the sacred symbols which have lost their symbolic character as pointers and have come

[2] See p. 176.

to claim meaning in their own right or the social structures and forms of civilization which have become self-sufficient are subjected to an ultimate criticism and shaken by catastrophe. When the prophetic spirit arises, when the relation of all existence to the ultimate source of meaning and existence becomes apparent in judgment, then the consciousness of Kairos and of the responsibility of man come to their climax.

Kairos is in a sense the antithesis of both Utopia and the Golden Age. A conservative theory of history finds all the meaning of history concentrated in the past; the present is significant insofar as it is related to that past. Utopianism finds the significance of the present in its relation to the future. But historical realism and relativism cannot make the significance of Greece and Rome depend on the contribution which they have been able to make to modern Western civilization or to some future Utopia. Neither can it find the significance of the present in the relative judgment which some future point in time will make of this period, or in the elements of modern culture which may survive or be selected by that future. It must see every period as somehow having its own meaning; yet its meaning cannot be intrinsic. It lies rather in the relation of an era to an ultimate that is beyond every point of time. The conception of Kairos expresses for Tillich both the negative meaning of historical relativism and the positive sense of the significance and responsibility of the present moment.

It is his conviction that we now stand in the Kairos, in the moment when the judgment of the eternal upon time and all things temporal and the responsibility of the temporal to the eternal become evident in the events of the period. We are facing not merely a transition from one stage of culture to another, from one religion to another. The problem of the present is not whether a communistic civilization will take the place of a capitalistic culture or whether a new faith will supplant Christianity. We are rather in a situation in which the whole question of the meaningfulness of existence is brought before us in such a fashion that we can not escape it, a period in which every social institution and religious symbol is challenged as to its right to existence. The eternal invades time and places every temporal form in question. There is in this not only judgment but also challenge to create such forms, such a culture and religion as will express the meaningfulness of all reality as a meaningfulness derived from the relation to the ultimate.

Tillich expects no reconstruction of life from sudden revolution. "When we look upon the actual events of our time," he writes, "must we not say that it seems as though a frost had fallen upon all of the things of which we have spoken, whether it be youth movement or the philosophy of life, whether it be expressionism or religious socialism? Was not all of this romanticism, intoxication, utopianism? One thing is certain: all of these things, and that means all of us also, are once more being subjected to the judgment. What was not real in what we did and thought is being consumed by fire. . . . And this means that the spirit of capitalist society is far too strong to be conquered by romanticism, longing and revolution. Its demonic power is too great. It means in the second place that the judgment which comes from the Unconditioned is not a dialectic but an extremely real power which drives us again and again to the verge of despair. And it means in the third place that in every sphere we must return to painstaking labor in the concrete situation."

It is evident that Tillich's interest in the philosophy of history is a practical interest. He is particularly active in the religious socialist movement and the practical as well as theoretic problem which he faces is the problem of combining socialism and religion. What he is seeking is not merely a coalition between a Christian idealism—which he would reject—and

socialist utopianism but a fundamental reinter-
pretation of the bases of socialism and a fundamental definition of the ethical task of religion.
Like Barth and Brunner and other members of
the dialectical school Tillich begins with the
ethical question, What shall I do? The theologians of crisis also began their course as religious
socialists and remain socialists to a large extent
to the present day. But the ethics to which the
logic of their theological position leads them appears to become more and more conservative.
They are in danger, as Tillich points out, of becoming supporters of things as they are, not because these things are good but because all reforms are also bad.[3] Tillich on the other hand
continues to assert the radical consequences of
the religious position and his whole theology
and philosophy must be approached from this
point of view among others. He is seeking for an
adequate philosophy of history and an adequate
social ethics.

His importance for English and American
readers lies largely in this fact. The ethics of
the "social gospel" of the past were mated with
naïve faith in progress and with a thoroughly
humanistic and anthropocentric religious atti-

[3] For Tillich's criticism of the theology of crisis, see pp. 217-
218. In more recent discussions he has become more critical
of this tendency.

tude. The decline of the liberal philosophy has called the whole social gospel into question. A change in the theological climate is evident. Will it be simple reaction, involving also the reaction to the orthodox conservative ethics? Liberalism and fundamentalism are equally intolerable, both in their theology and in their ethics. The struggle for a new theology and a radical ethics of the Christian life is inevitable in England and America as well as in Germany. In this struggle Tillich's point of view can be very helpful. The crisis is naturally more acute and the problems are more sharply defined in Germany than elsewhere, not only because the German temper runs to sharp antitheses and exclusive definitions but also because that country has been visited by a severer fate in our time than the other countries of the West have been. Nevertheless the problems of religious socialism, of the reconstruction of Protestantism and of the religious foundations of the new culture are pressing for solution in England and America also. Because this is true and because the present book offers illuminating points of view and provocative interpretations it is offered in translation.

Acknowledgment and thanks are due to Professor Tillich and to Mr. Herman J. Sander for their aid in the work of translation. Mr. Sander furnished the first draft of the English version of the second chapter but the translator of the book must accept responsibility for the accuracy and the intelligibility of the translation as a whole.

H. RICHARD NIEBUHR

AUTHOR'S PREFACE

A book on the religious situation of the present must deal with the whole contemporary world, for there is nothing that is not in some way the expression of the religious situation. But it is impossible for any one to write about all contemporary things; we can make serious and worth-while statements about things only in so far as we have had vital contact with them. This does not mean that the limitations imposed upon us are those of the specialist. To contemplate things from the point of view of eternity does not mean to regard them with the eyes of the specialist, not even of the theological specialist. It means rather that they are to be studied for the sake of discovering what they signify for the relation of our time to eternity. It is impossible however to do this unless we are vitally identified with them. Hence the limitation of all seriously meant statements about them. These limitations do not obtain for the reader in the same way as they do for the writer; the former's boundaries of vital contact with things will lie elsewhere. The difficulty is inescapable but it will be salutary if its result be that the reader on his part, stimulated by his contradictions and assents, lets his own relations to life and reality develop their meaning.

References to literature have been wholly omitted; in view of the large number of fields touched upon they would have grown to infinity. For a discussion such as the present one, it is not literature but rather one's own criticism and one's own vital and responsible participation in the life of the present-day world which are of decisive importance.

Many a reader will be able to understand the exposition more easily if he will proceed from the introduction to the third chapter, then to the second and finally to the section on science and metaphysics.

Not only the choice of material but also the position from which it is judged depend ultimately upon a personal decision. The attentive reader will not fail to discover the position of the author for it is presented plainly enough. Any so-called objective interpretation of the present is in part a self-delusion, in part bore-dom. Yet I trust that my position is really a position, not merely a subjective and therefore arbitrary collection of opinions. A responsible and creative criticism of one's own time is possi-ble only on the basis of a real position and not by means either of a specious objectivity or of an arbitrary subjectivity.

One misunderstanding must be guarded against from the beginning; the *spirit of capi-talist society,* which occupies a central place in the following discussion does not mean the spirit of individual men or of a class or a party. It is rather a symbol for an ultimate, fundamental attitude toward the world. It is, to be sure, a very real symbol and in our situation it is most concretely visible in actual, capitalist society, whence it derives its name. But it means some-thing far wider than this society.

If the book succeeds in bearing effective testi-mony to the shaking of this spirit and hence to the shaking of our time by eternity it will have fulfilled its purpose.

PAUL TILLICH

INTRODUCTION

INTRODUCTION

is such a thing as spiritual perspective, the possibility of finding amid all the infinite aspirations and tensions which every present contains not only those which conserve the past but also those which are creatively new and pregnant with the future. There is such a thing as apprehension of the growing form, just as there is an apprehension of the grand outlines of past development. To understand the present means ultimately to understand the future with which the womb of the present is great. But if spirit is direction, tension toward the future, then every outlook toward the future from the point of view of the present is also necessarily directed and tense, in short, the outlook of a creative will, not merely of indifferent observation. Whoever would maintain the ideal of pure observation must content himself with numbers and names, statistics and newspaper clippings. He might collect thousands of things which could be verified but he would not for that reason be able to understand what is actually happening in the present. One is enabled to speak of that which is most vital in the present, of that which makes the present a generative force, only insofar as one immerses oneself in the creative process which brings the future forth out of the past.

Such a view must appear to be extremely subjective and arbitrary unless one understands the

ONE

THE PRESENT AND THE RELIGIOUS SITUATION

We are to deal with the religious situation of the present day. Before we approach the subject itself we must pause for a moment to think about the topic and its terms. Such a procedure may enable us to enter into our subject more immediately and profoundly than would be possible if we made the direct approach. For the formulation of a topic is itself the result of long intellectual labors and sometimes it is a very questionable and problematical result. This is true in our case.

We are to deal with the religious situation of the present—in some way, then, with the *present*. Questions begin to arise at once. How is it possible to speak of the present when the present is a nothing, a boundary between past and

future, a line without any breadth, on which
nothing can stand and about which, therefore,
nothing can be said? For this reason every one
who tries to speak about the present inevitably
tends to speak rather of the past, near or remote,
and of the future, most distant or most near.
And some, indeed, who try to speak about the
present discover that they are speaking of none
of these three times but of the eternity which is
above all times. Thus we have three answers to
our question about the nature of the present:
the present is the past, the present is the future,
and the present is eternity. We need first of all
to study these three answers.

The present is the past. Every present movement is a wave which has been raised by the
waves of all the past. It is an individual event,
to be sure; it is unique; but the individual event
has received its content from and is borne along
by the infinity of other things, by the past.
Hence the eye cannot remain fixed on this one
thing; the more profoundly it penetrates into
the nature of the object the more it tends to
glide, consciously or unconsciously, toward the
past—first toward the nearest other event, from
there to the more distant and, if it were possible,
to all other events. The present is what it is only
in union with all that has gone before and without this other-than-itself, on which it rests, it is

nothing. How, then, can anything be asserted i
every assertion must assert everything? Our
senses help themselves out of a similar difficulty
in their observation of the external world by the
use of a simple device—perspective. As it is in
the world of space so it is also in the world of
time. Only the figures which are very near are
clearly visible; the farther the figures are removed the simpler their outlines become until
at last they fade from view. Without perspective no object can be seen in its right spatial or
temporal location. And this is even truer of the
world of spiritual realities than it is of the world
of things. For the spiritual achieves individuality only insofar as it contains affirmation and
denial of other individuals. Knowledge of a spir
itual phenomenon means apprehension of it
affirmation and denial of other spiritual phe
nomena. To understand the present means
apprehend its affirmations and denials of t
past, near and remote.

Now for the second answer: the present is t
future. To live in the present is to live in t
sion toward the future; every present is ess
tially a transition out of the past into the futu
Spirit or mind is always direction from t
which is to that which ought to be. To un
stand the present means to see it in its i
tension toward the future. In this field also t

third answer, the statement that the present is eternity. This alone is the real and final reply to our question and at the same time the one which carries us into the heart of our subject. For surely it would not be worth while to speak at all of the fact that all sorts of things, ideas or feelings or deeds or works, move out of the past into the future across the mysterious boundary line of the present if all this were nothing but a moving, a flowing, a becoming and decaying without ultimate meaning or final importance. All of this is really important if it has an unconditioned meaning, an unconditioned depth, an unconditioned reality. That it possesses this unconditioned meaning cannot be made a matter of proof or disproof but only of faith in the unconditioned meaning of life. Unless some spark of that faith is present there can be no spirit; for to live spiritually is to live in the presence of meaning and without an ultimate meaning everything disappears into the abyss of meaninglessness. To speak of an unconditioned meaning is to speak of that which transcends the process of mere becoming, the mere transition from past to future; it is to speak of that which supports the times but is not subject to them. If any present has meaning it has eternity. Only because the present is eternity does it possess a significance which makes its study worth while. We may therefore combine our three questions and inquire after the eternal which presses on out of the past, in and through the present, toward future actualization.

This question transports us to the heart of our subject, that is to say, it raises the problem of the religious situation of the present. Yet we may pause once more to inquire into the meaning of the term *religious situation*. Religion deals with a relation of man to the eternal. But a relation has two sides; hence two answers can be given as we take the point of view either of the temporal or of the eternal. The first answer, which proceeds from the temporal and human, will speak of tendencies in specifically religious affairs, of churches, sects, theologies and all sorts of accompanying religious movements. Doubtless these things must be considered if the religious situation of a period is to be understood. But the questionable element in this procedure is that attention is given to just those things with which religion itself is not concerned, to the stream of events hastening out of the past into the future, while the real meaning and content of that stream, the eternal to which all things refer, is neglected. If the question be reversed so that one begins with the other side of religion, with the eternal and divine, it gains a far more comprehensive and fundamental significance. It has now become a question about the situation of a period in all its relations and phenomena, about its essential meaning, about the eternal which is present in a time. Human religion from this point of view is only a part of the total phenomenon; it is that part which testifies to the ultimate meaning and which has been especially called to do so since by nature it seeks to be in relation to the eternal. But it is not the only phenomenon which bears witness to the ultimate and in some periods it is not even the most important of the witnesses or the most effective in expression and symbolism. Every spiritual phenomenon of a period expresses its eternal content and one of the most important characteristics of a time has been defined when we have discovered which of the various aspects of culture is most expressive of its real meaning.

When we raise the question about the religious situation of the present in this comprehensive sense one answer, which is applicable to all periods and which applies, therefore, to our own, offers itself at once. Every period of time, since it is time, is self-sufficient in its forms, in its existential content, in its vital tendencies; yet it is not possible for any time to be self-sufficient. Because it is time there is something within it which drives it beyond itself at every moment, not toward the future, which would be only a new time with the same impossibility of being self-sufficient, but toward something which is no longer time. The fact that it is impossible for existence to rest content with itself and its forms is revealed best of all in the profound, catastrophic movements in reality where that which is really creative is at work. For the real creations of every time speak of something that is not time. And the most profound revelations of existence testify to something that is not an existence. Whenever a period speaks most effectively and clearly of itself it speaks no longer of itself but of something else, of a reality which lies beneath all time and above all existential forms. The real miracle of time and of every present is not only that it can transcend itself but that as a result of unpredictable catastrophes it must transcend itself ever and again. That is one aspect of the religious situation of every present, that is, in relation to the eternal.

Returning now to the other side, which we made our point of departure, we may say that time lives within itself and its forms and because the eternal is taken up into the forms of time it becomes an existential form, temporal and contemporary. The Other, that in which every time transcends itself, becomes an individual event, a present in time. That which is not time becomes time, that which is not an existential form becomes an existing form. This is the other aspect of the religious situation of a time, of its situation as time in the presence of the eternal. We find self-transcendence in every time, openness to the eternal, a hallowing of time; but upon the other hand we see the appropriation of the eternal, the self-sufficiency of time, the secularization of the holy. There is a movement to and fro between self-transcendence and self-sufficiency, between the desire to be a mere vessel and to the desire to be the content, between the turning toward the eternal and the turning toward the self. In this action and reaction we discern the religious situation of every present at its profoundest level.

Where now shall we find that existent reality, the time, the present, about which all this is to be said? Doubtless it is not to be found in nature with its cyclical process, its distant and strange past and its distant and strange future. Society is the carrier of the existing present as an historical reality; it is the existent thing which we are inquiring after in this context. A religious situation is always at the same time the situation of a society. But the term *situation* seems to mean something which is established, at rest and constant, a basic fact which lies at a deeper level than do all the visible tendencies, something which is invisible to those who live within it but which is, for that reason, all the more effective. It refers to an unconscious, self-evident faith which lies at a deeper level than the apparent antithesis of the belief and unbelief which both arise out of it and are both equally rooted in it. This unconscious faith which is not assailed because it is the presupposition of life and is lived rather than thought of, this all-determining, final source of meaning constitutes the actual religious situation of a period. We must attempt to penetrate through to this faith.

Yet it must be conceded at the outset that this attempt is subject to certain essential limitations. Not every situation, not every society, can be understood from the point of view of another situation or society; but only that one which is vitally related to the one from which it is observed. Hence the present about which we can speak is the life of our Western society. Even this society is divided and is cut across by creedal and national walls which it is difficult for individuals to surmount. To concede this does not mean that we are limiting ourselves intentionally but that there are actual limitations which can never be wholly transcended and of which one must remain conscious, particularly when one's point of view is located in the midst of deeply shaken mid-European society.

TWO

THE RELIGIOUS SITUATION OF CAPITALIST SOCIETY IN THE NINETEENTH CENTURY

Our contemporary religious situation has been influenced decisively by recent revolts against the spiritual situation and the social forms which prevailed during the closing decades of the nineteenth century. These revolts, after some prophetic fore-runners had prepared the way, began at about the turn of the century and developed their full force in the nineteen twenties. If we would understand their significance it will be necessary to sketch in outline the meaning of that Western spiritual and social situation which we call typically capitalist or bourgeois.

For this purpose we must inquire what the spiritually powerful, the really representative, products of that period were. There were three

41

of these: mathematical natural science, technique and capitalist economy. These three belong together, for science is a servant of technique in which it also celebrates its greatest triumphs while technique is a servant of the economy and makes possible the development of a world-embracing economic system. The carrier of this three-fold activity, which is in turn supported and established by it, is capitalist society. It is easy to show how everything else was made serviceable to this trinity—first of all, science itself. The sciences of mind or spirit were forced to abdicate in favor of the natural sciences; when one spoke of spiritual facts one regarded them as natural processes taking place within the genus man. Psychology, which was treated as a department of natural science, claimed to be the fundamental science of spirit. To history was committed the task of ascertaining facts of the past but it was not granted the rank of an exact science. Philosophy cautiously withdrew to the examination of logical and methodological questions for the sake of providing bases for science while metaphysics declared the fundamental scientific concepts—the concept of the atom and the laws of its motions—to be the essence of all things. Art and literature labored to present scientifically accurate representations of every sort of reality or, with brilliant command of forms, they sought to set forth the momentary impressions which external nature makes upon internal nature, the soul (Realism and Impressionism).

In political life the national state was drawn, externally and internally, into the service of economics. It was forgotten that the idea of nationalism which stirred the nineteenth century so mightily contained in its essence a profound contradiction to the scientific tendency toward abstract concepts and to the universal, rational state which science demanded. All the bonds of original, organic community life must be sacrificed in favor of a free capitalist economy. The right and might of the state are placed at the disposal of the capitalist class for the control of the proletarian masses which it dominates. Not only in internal affairs but also in foreign relations the state with all its agencies for the exercise of its powers and with its steadily increasing armaments serves the expansive, imperialist will of the leading economic class. As it is in the political life so it is also in the social life. Capitalist society, even according to the definition of the concept, is a human group analyzable after the fashion of natural science into pure individuals—the atoms of society—which are held together by economic purposes and needs—the natural laws of capitalist society. Conflict and solidarity of interests are the decisive forces in this process of grouping. Classes and class-struggles arise. Cultural education becomes the hall mark of a class and an instrument of economic power. Even the ethical ideal becomes more and more subservient to the economic end; the fundamental virtues in the ethics of capitalist society are economic efficiency, developed to the utmost degree of ruthless activity, on the part of the leaders, submissive acceptance of their place in the great machine of the whole economic life on the part of those led, obedient subjection on the part of all to the conventions of bourgeois custom and, along with these, impersonal charity for the support of the economically helpless.

The churches were powerless in the face of this development. The Reformed Protestantism of England, America, Holland and western Germany entered into alliance with the economic ethics of capitalism at an early date. Lutheranism stood and still stands aloof from it but by a round-about way through state ecclesiasticism and the sanctification of the national will-to-power it became possibly even more dependent on capitalism than Calvinism had become. The Catholic church remained in the moderate opposition but was persistently forced aside until it entered into a loose alliance with the social opponents of capitalism. In the field of theory the churches were able to maintain their independence somewhat more definitely than in the practical sphere. It was natural that all of them should carry on an emphatic controversy with materialistic metaphysics. Many other consequences of the naturalistic view of the world, as for instance the doctrine of evolution, were also rejected for a long time. But in this case as in others the churches retreated step by step. Protestant theology united with the critical Kantian philosophy, recognized modern science without any reservations and claimed for itself as its exclusive field the realm of faith, in the firm confidence that it was relieved in this way of all further conflict with science. It was a retreat, a retirement along the whole line, which, to be sure, saved religious life from utter destruction but reduced it by and large to a mere side-issue. The lofty claims whereby it was maintained as a national or popular faith in state and people's churches were quite out of proportion to its actual significance.

It would be a highly unfair, abstract and untrue interpretation, to be sure, were one to ignore the fact that even in the nineteenth century numerous revolts arose against the spirit of capitalist society. The century began with the great period of idealism and romanticism and their many-sided protests against the spirit of naturalism and of the Illumination. Despite the severe spiritual catastrophe in the thirties which marked the end of this period its influences were noticeable throughout the nineteenth century. Yet the fact that the strongest forces which the idealistic and romantic movement aroused —national patriotism, the religious awakening and the historical consciousness—were slowly but surely destroyed or attached by the technological, economic spirit, bears witness to the latter's overpowering force.

Among the Western nations Russia was the source of a constant opposition to the dominance of capitalist society. A peculiar religious sense of a vocation to save the West grew up in that country during the period. But no attention was really paid to this opposition until much later in the twentieth century and after the naturalistic and economic spirit in the form of a Marxist revolution had won a tremendous victory in Russia also. Externally it was the greatest victory of all.

How hopeless all opposition was at the end of the nineteenth century is shown with terrible clarity by the fate of three great warriors against the prevailing spirit and prophets of coming things: Nietzsche, Strindberg and van Gogh. The philosopher, the poet and the painter, all three, were broken mentally and spiritually in their desperate struggle with the spirit of capitalist society. Thus even the movements of opposition at the beginning and the end of the last century bear witness in defeat to the victory of the trinity of natural science, technique and capitalist economy, to the triumph of the spirit of capitalist society.

What now is the meaning of such a spiritual situation? What is its significance from the point of view of our question about the relationship of time and eternity? Evidently it is an extreme example of a self-assertive, self-sufficient type of existence. This applies to mathematical natural science which pursues the goal of demonstrating that reality is governed wholly by its own laws and is rationally intelligible and which keeps its distance from that region where reason is shaken by skepticism at the inner and outer limits of mathematical calculation. It applies to world-ruling technique with its will to conquer space, time and nature and to make the earth a well-furnished dwelling of man. It applies, finally, to capitalist economy which seeks to provide the greatest possible number of men with the greatest possible amount of economic goods, which seeks to arouse and to satisfy ever increasing demands without raising the question as to the meaning of the process which claims the service of all the spiritual and physical human abilities. In all of this there is no trace of self-transcendence, of the hallowing of existence. The forms of the life-process have become completely independent of the source of life and its meaning. They are self-sufficient and produce a self-sufficient present. And all phases of life which are subject to the spirit of rationalistic science, technique and economy bear witness to the time as one which is self-sufficient, which affirms itself and its finitude.

Yet it is impossible to rest content with such an evaluation. For is not the eternal the unseen support even of a time which turns away from it? If it were not so no time could exist. Even the way in which existence turned back upon itself in the three phases which have been described was an effect of past devotion to the eternal. The mathematical natural science of Kepler, Galilei and Newton was born out of the desire to know the laws of God's creation, to understand matter as revealing the creator's glory and rationality after it had been regarded since the times of the Greeks as something inferior and anti-divine. Only after the desire to find God in nature had been lost did science turn profane and become the sphere in which resistance was offered to the questions and doubts which proceed from the eternal. Victorious technique was originally an agency for the emanci-

pation of man from the demonic powers in all
natural things. It was a revelation of the power
of spirit over matter. It was and it remains for
innumerable people a means of deliverance
from a stupid, beastlike existence. To a large
extent it is the fulfillment of that which the
Utopias of Renaissance philosophers dreamed
of as a kingdom of reason and of the control of
nature. Similarly, liberal economy and capitalist
society, which this technique supports, were
based upon the emancipation and the high evaluation of the individual and his creative powers. Countless shackles needed to be broken,
countless means of oppression to be eliminated,
in order that bourgeois society, i.e. the society
of independent, autonomous individuals, might
arise. The motive power in this emancipation
came out of the recognition of the sacredness of
personality, out of faith in human rights and human worth. The power and superiority of capitalist society lie in the fact that it contains these
values. It did not turn away from this which was
its eternal meaning until emancipated personality engaging in the conflicts of capitalist economy had been filled with unlimited desire for
economic power and until free competition had
forced upon almost all social groups an un-
bounded striving after profits and so the war of
all against all. Only after this had happened did

liberal economy with the technique which supported it become the most powerful symbol of a self-seeking, time-fettered existence. Then it became for many, particularly for the masses, which were oppressed as a result of the conflict, not only a profane but also a demonic and antidivine symbol.

The last observations have clearly shown how an historical process may be dominated by the rhythm of holy and profane, of eternal and temporal, how in life devotion to the eternal can turn into denial, into the profanization of what was originally holy, how it can turn even into a demonic antithesis to the divine. We are not dealing however with an arbitrarily selected period of history but with that period on which our own lives are founded and the significance of which is not diminished by the fact that we are moving away from it. We come out of a time in which existence was directed toward itself, in which the forms of life were self-sufficient and closed against invasions of the eternal. Not a single phase of that life out of which we have come, not even the explicitly religious phase, was exempt from this attitude. Even the forces which assailed it became its victims. We come out of a time which no longer possessed any symbols by which it could point beyond itself. Capitalist society rested undisturbed in its finite form.

That situation has been destroyed. The time has experienced shocks which it could not resist, the effects of which it could neither reject nor secularize. Not only war and revolution brought about these shocks. Even before these occurred internal revolts against the spirit of capitalist society had begun all along the line and had led, in the younger generation, to decisive transformations. War and revolution accelerated the development but they did not in any essential way interfere with its constancy. Hence we may include the entire first quarter of the twentieth century in our study.

We are to speak of the situation of this period in its relation to eternity. Therein we see the real religious situation of the present. We will not confine our attention therefore to intra-religious movements but shall begin with a comprehensive study of all aspects of the spiritual and social life. Whoever wants to understand the religious situation of the present must make his first researches at this point. It is not an accident that this is necessary. For just as it was the non-ecclesiastical culture which had almost exclusively held the leadership in the previous century so also it was out of this culture that the

revolutionary movements of the twentieth century arose. The churches followed very slowly
and contributed creative power at very few
points. The total movement with which we are
concerned is the slowly developing defeat of the
spiritual temper of the nineteenth century. The
self-sufficient this-worldliness of capitalist culture and religion is being disturbed. Questions
and doubts are arising on all sides; they point
toward something beyond time and threaten
the security of a present which has cut itself
loose from the eternal. Doubt is cast on the complete rationality of the three great powers, science, technique and capitalist economy; abysses
are opening on all sides and everywhere the
souls of men are struggling for fulfillments
which must arise out of the deeper strata of life.
The struggle is not always successful; the forces
of a time directed toward itself, of rationalism
and of mechanism, are too strong. How should
it be possible, indeed, to conquer in one assault
the forces which have claimed the minds and
souls of men for almost five hundred years!
Nevertheless some victories are won, above all
the victory of the conviction that this struggle
dare not be abandoned until a present time is
at hand which is resolved to make its own existence and its forms the vessels of an eternal
meaning.

Of these struggles, defeats and victories we are to speak. They constitute the religious situation of our time. We shall deal first of all with the theoretical aspect of the spiritual life, under which head we include science, art and metaphysics; we shall proceed to the practical aspect, to which economy, politics, the social and the ethical life belong; we shall turn, finally, to the explicitly religious movements within and outside the churches.

THE PRESENT RELIGIOUS SITUATION IN THE SPHERES OF SCIENCE AND ART

ONE

SCIENCE

I. The Vital and the Structure. Unshaken in its fundamental methodology and probably unshakable for an unpredictably long period of future time mathematical natural science stands firm and with it everything which influences its method. Even the modern theory of relativity has not changed that fact. It is to be evaluated, rather, as the climax of the whole development. By eliminating every absolute point of reference for the calculation of movements it has aided the mathematical tendency to achieve a complete victory. Yet it has disturbed somewhat the consciousness of the physical sciences. It has revealed more clearly than was previously apparent the infinity of existence, which always offers the same constant results to mathematical abstraction, to be sure, but which shrouds its true nature in deeper mystery than before.

Awareness of the irrationality of the existent has become more acute on another side also. The philosophy of life, which had been influenced strongly by Nietzsche, has set forth in very impressive fashion the distinction between creative life and petrifying calculation. Bergson in France and Simmel in Germany have restored to life its right to be considered as a primal and original datum and have characterized mathematical abstraction as the secondary and derivative element. In doing this Bergson confined himself to biology and psychology while Simmel went beyond this sphere to sociology, ethics, esthetics and religion. Now the way into the profounder levels of life is not to be found by means of physical and psychological analysis but only by means of intuitive insight, of apprehension of the basis of one's own aliveness. It is inevitable that in this procedure the meaningful ground of things, when it is really touched, should reveal itself as their relation to the eternal or as their religious content. It is the creative and inexhaustible ground of reality which has been rediscovered by the philosophy of life.

The special sciences also contributed toward the development of this tendency. The old conflict in biology over the question whether the vital could be explained in terms of the non-living, of atoms and their organization, or whether a separate sphere of life, a vital force or something of that sort, needed to be assumed, was decided ever more frequently in favor of the latter alternative. It was understood—however the detailed explanation ran—that the living organism was the primary fact and that physical and chemical processes were secondary. This did not mean that physical and chemical analyses were to be restricted, for the vital principle is not useful for the explanation of details. It meant, rather, that life needed to be seen as the presupposition of all the processes which go on within it. The decisive point was the recognition that a living structure cannot be composed out of its parts but can only grow forth out of an original, creative source.

The concept of structure (*Gestalt*) which arose in biology reacted upon physical science. In the analysis of matter it becomes ever more apparent that in the inorganic world also structure rather than lack of structure is the primary fact. The structures of crystals, even of molecules and finally of atoms, with their polar tensions between nuclei and orbital electrons, were revealed. And just as the exploration of the infinitely small discovered structure so also the astronomical observation of the infinitely great revealed ever more of structure in the apparently irregular and accidental universe of the fixed stars. Contingency on the one hand, rational necessity on the other hand—these were the two concepts in which the meaninglessness of that picture of a self-sufficient world which the past epoch had constructed were most clearly expressed. But the combination of creative freedom and meaningful structure expressed the reference of existence to the eternal ground of meaning.

In the field of medicine the doctrine of structure achieved practical significance to an increasing degree. The study of disease from the point of view of the total organism and the effort to exercise healing influences upon the central functions of life are becoming more important in comparison with specialist attention to the individual organ and the individual process. And this is true not only of the external aspects of the living structure but also of its internal aspects, the psychical life.

In the wide field of psychology the concept of structure and the method of inner, intuitive understanding have won victory upon victory. The soul also had been analyzed into atoms and the laws of their motion—that is, into sensations and the laws of their association. But even Wundt, the master of German psychology, had shown that the decisive events of the psychical life are dependent on a creative act which cannot be derived from the psychical elements. Modern psychology (Köhler, Wertheimer, Spranger) has recognized that no individual psychical process can be dealt with in abstraction from the total psychical structure but that the whole is present in every moment of inner experience and that, further, the mind apprehends realities not piece by piece but as wholes. The psychical in general and the individual soul in particular are primary creative structures which are apprehensible in their unity and vitality only by means of intuition. But wherever the creative character of a reality is intuited there the way to the original, creative ground has been opened.

The emancipation of psychology from domination by physiology has been particularly important for this development. No one can seriously doubt the dependence of the psychical upon the physical. But the real problem is how this dependence is to be explained. The experimental method in psychology guaranteed extraordinary preponderance to the physical and obscured the independent, structural character of the psychical. Medical science made a decisive assault upon this position. The psycho-analytical school of the Viennese physician Freud achieved insights into the springs of the psychical organism which seriously impaired the dogma of the physical basis of all psychical disorders and made possible the development of the purely psychological therapeutic method of psycho-analysis. This discovery was important ethically and religiously particularly because it recognized—with questionable over-emphasis, to be sure—the fundamental importance of the erotic sphere for all aspects of the psychical life. It was an insight of which religion has ever been aware and which only the conventions of bourgeois society have relegated to the limbo of forgotten truth. It was not accidental, therefore, that psychological literature took up this problem and after a vehement struggle forced the recognition of its importance. Speaking in the language of religion, psycho-analysis and the literature allied with it cast light upon the demonic background of life. But wherever the demonic appears there the question as to its correlate, the divine, will also be raised. Speaking psycho-analytically, this is the question as to the power which can sublimate the erotic drive present in all things psychical.

Sociology is closely related to psychology insofar as the former is conceived not vaguely as the science of the whole culture which society supports, but definitely and clearly as the science of the forms of the social process. In sociology there has been a development also from the concept of atom to the concept of structure. It was scarcely to be avoided that capitalist society should regard itself as an association of individuals united for the sake of common production, that it should begin with the idea of a structureless multiplicity. For that is the character of capitalist society. But even this society is able to exist only because there are effective within it general social forces which it did not produce but upon which it is dependent. Even in capitalist society sociological structure is the primary fact and the never quite successful tendency toward disintegration the second fact. The structural character of sociological entities is being recognized not only by the romantic and reactionary sociology of Ottmar Spann but also by the more realistic theory of Vierkandt, which approaches the idea of structure very hesitatingly and which is therefore the more significant for our argument. The point at which the reference of existence to the eternal becomes apparent in sociological thought is the same point at which this reference appears in psychology and biology—at the absolute givenness, the underivability, the inconstruability of the living structure, the non-rational ground on which this structure rests and which comes to expression in the demonic-divine polarity of conflict and social integration, of the will-to-power and love. These things, to be sure, are rarely seen in their essential character, in their reference to the eternal, and a justifiable realism in sociology as in biology will offer determined resistance to those romantic reactions which are always merely disguised defeats.

In many ways sociology like psychology remains an obstacle to a clear-cut distinction between the sciences of mind or spirit and the sciences which deal with the carriers of spirit, soul and society. In this also there is evidence of the dominance of bourgeois society which wants to be at rest in its own forms and does not want to feel the pangs of the spirit.

II. *The Individual and the Spirit.* "Spirit is life which itself cutteth into life," said Nietzsche. This deep inwardness of the spirit, this pain of the spiritual, reveals that wherever there is spirit there the self-sufficiency of existence has been shattered. Therefore the battle for the eternal is always at the same time a battle for the spirit. It is more than this but it is this also. Hence the status of the battle for the spirit is one of the most significant symptoms of the religious situation of a period.

It began to be recognized in philosophy that the method of scientific abstraction necessarily ignored one aspect of reality, the individual. For the method which seeks general laws must abstract from individual events. But the spiritual never appears to us save in individual form, as the history of creative individual events. Science on the contrary seems to demand universality and exact conformity to law. Consequently alternative methods of procedure offered themselves: either history could be excluded from the sphere of the genuine sciences or the effort could be made to introduce into history the method of explanation by general laws. In view of the great progress in historical knowledge and of the development of rigorous methods of historical research the first of these ways became impossible. The second way alone remained open; it led to the controversy about historical methodology which developed during the first decade of this century. Is it possible to understand history as one apprehends a physical process, as developing in accordance with general laws, or do we deal in history with unique, non-derivable processes which can only be observed and described? While the great historian Lamprecht adopted the former position theoretically and above all in practice, philosophy, especially as represented by Rickert, with the support of many historians successfully defended the second position. Actual historical composition contradicted the generalizing method too emphatically for the latter to be able to prevail. Individual, creative mind triumphed over general law and it was possible for Troeltsch to build systematically on the newly conquered ground in his *Historism and Its Problems*. His discussions clearly indicate what religious significance attaches to this turn toward the individual and creative. Once more history contains something that is underived, unique and revealed.

In the nineteenth century Dilthey had struggled heroically to work out an adequate methodology for the social and spiritual sciences. He discovered the concept of "historical understanding" and applied the method of historical understanding with an unexcelled mastery. To understand means to enter into the nature of a strange, living structure. This concept is also fundamentally a polemical weapon, directed against the analyzing and generalizing method of the natural sciences which does not seek to understand but to explain. The extensive and increasing influence which Dilthey has exercised has come to be highly important for the growth of insight into the independent and underived character of the spiritual life. Very largely because of these influences materialism has disappeared almost completely from the general cultural consciousness.

Historical insight was lifted to a higher plane under the influence of poetic intuition by the philosophical disciples of Stefan George. A directly religious influence was noticeable in the thought—advanced particularly by Bertram in the preface of his book on Nietzsche—that when they are historically regarded great spiritual figures become mythical characters. Myth, however, is a specifically religious category. Two things are implied in the thought; upon the one hand it is implied that the observing spirit when it exercises historical understanding is more than a blank tablet which receives clear or vague impressions of a foreign and determinate reality. When spirit understands spirit it interprets at the same time. The object receives a meaning which is born out of the interaction of that which understands with that which is understood. Thus historical understanding comes to be a function of life through which the past receives meaning from the present and the present from the past. The spirit is not a thing which can be studied by spirit without undergoing alteration; spirit yields itself, sacrifices itself and becomes creative in its contact with spirit. The statement that the intuition of historical essences is mythical implies something further. Mythical means symbolical of the eternal. To view an historical figure mythically means to re-gard it as the expression of a meaning which is rooted in the depth of the eternal; it means in the last analysis to regard it religiously. One cannot suppress the objection to the theory of the George school that myth—just because it breaks through the boundaries of the rational sphere—is a growth and cannot be manufac-tured. Great creative writing of history will al-ways be marked by mythologizing tendencies, whether or not it desires them. But lesser tal-ents will not succeed because they speak of myths; on the contrary they are likely to fall victim to fantastic and barren cleverness. De-feats of this sort on the voyage from the past into the future will probably remain unavoida-ble for a long time.

The independence of the spiritual is becom-ing patent to an ever increasing degree. Further evidence for that fact is to be found in the rise and growing importance of the history of spirit —of mind and culture—in distinction from gen-eral history. The history of spirit is the history of the spiritual creations, not insofar as they ex-ist but insofar as they are meaningful. Its pur-pose is to understand the relations of meaning which connect spiritual movements. But the complex structure of meaning can be interpreted only from the point of view of an apprehension of meaning, that is, from a personal standpoint, from one's own normative idea. Hence the history of spirit is closely related to the constructive, systematic sciences of spirit or mind. Indeed the constructive effort often proceeds by means of historical understanding of classic figures of the past—an indication of the extent to which insight into the nature of spirit and its original, creative character dominates historical thought.

Of decisive importance for the science of spirit is its relation to psychology. The most serious threats to the independence of the life of the spirit arose at this point; here the conflict was most severe but the victory also most decisive. Strangely enough the change came out of psychology itself. Dilthey in his time had sought to differentiate between explanatory and descriptive psychology; while explanation analyzes into elements which it then seeks to recombine, description directs attention to the unified living structure and its members. These ideas, however, became really important only after they were combined with logical elements derived from mathematics. Husserl's *Logical Studies* which began to appear in 1900 furnished a critique of psychologism and led to the recognition, rarely challenged to-day, that the mind is independent of the psychical processes in which it actualizes itself. Indeed, the doctrine of intentional mental acts and their necessary relation to the spheres of value subordinated psychical process itself to value and to contingency upon the spiritual. Just at the critical point of the relation of nature and spirit, therefore, the spirit is asserting its own independent meaning with increasing effectiveness and with spirit the denial of the absoluteness of the world of existences comes to expression.

III. *Philosophy and Method.* Philosophy is the direct self-expression of a period in the theoretic sphere. Because it transcends the special sciences and is yet most intimately connected with each of them the most general element in the scientific attitude comes to appearance in it, the element which arises out of levels deeper than science and which relates to the whole man, to the whole of a period. This element is expressed less in the specific details of scientific knowledge than in the philosophic method. For method is to philosophy what style is to art, the expression of the intellectual attitude of the individual and of the spiritual situation of the whole.

The philosophic method which corresponded, positively as well as negatively, to bourgeois society was the critical method. The dominance of the pure rational form, the subjection of nature, the emancipation of autonomous personality, were all implied in this method which received its classic formulation in Kant. At the same time, however, it implied the isolation of the individual, the inner impoverishment of nature and the social life and bondage to the closed world of forms in which all critical thought is interested. On the one side it is a heroic philosophy, supported by a strong ethics, on the other side it is the expression of the never-ending relation of all thought and action to the finite world, a relation which is always bound to the finite.

The attack against the purely critical method which arose on all sides was directed against both its positive and its negative aspects. The subjection of everything to the purely rational form was attacked as formalism; everywhere the effort was made to break the bondage to the closed system of forms. "Beyond Kant" became the common watchword of the most diverse movements. At the present time, when this goal has been largely reached, the attempt is being made to destroy the critical interpretation of Kant's philosophy and to show that the tendencies to transcend the critical Kant were present even in Kant himself. The previously unknown writings of Kant's old age offer the best evidence for this contention.

It was naturally suggested that in seeking a way beyond Kant one trace the same path which his immediate successors pursued. The German idealistic philosophy, on which the nineteenth century had heaped its scorn and which had almost been forgotten, was rediscovered and won increasing influence; Fichte, Hegel, Schelling and Fries won disciples and continue to win them. The motives in the movement are mixed; among them were the imposing power of Fichte's personality, his deeply grounded patriotism, the mystical character of his *Way to the Blessed Life*, the greatness and coherence of Hegel's thought, the power of his conceptualizations, the universalism and concreteness of his philosophy, the depth and esthetic charm of Schelling's romantic thought, and, finally, the brilliant manner in which Fries, while remaining very close to Kant, made the transition to intuition. All these interests, varying according to personal temperament or even according to the more or less accidental contact of individuals with the literature, made deep impressions on many representatives of the new generation which arose after 1900. It seemed certain that this philosophy, orientated toward spirit and the eternal, was to win a speedy victory. But the spirit chose a different way. The catastrophe which idealism had suffered in the nineteenth century had been too terrible for any one to invite its recurrence. The fundamental attitude of the time was too strongly realistic to be able to yield to an idealism which was unwilling to bear the burdens of the day. For what had brought about the first catastrophe of idealism and would have led to a second was just this, that it cannot see the true religious situation, the situation of time in the presence of eternity, that it seeks to evade the judgment under which the temporal stands before the eternal. Its forms, to be sure, are open to the reception of the living content, it restores to the state and even to logic their primordial and essential holiness, but it rests content then with these sanctified forms; it does not penetrate to the absolutely transcendent, to that which lies beyond even the most sacred form, whether it be called church or state; it does not see the abyss which opens before every time and every present. For this reason positive theology and critical philosophy have become allies in common opposition to the return of idealism. Above all, however, the social and political events of the time make a new idealistic, romantic philosophy impossible. War and revolution have revealed depths of reality which idealism cannot master.

Yet renascent idealism prepared the way for a series of movements which pursued similar goals though they traveled by different, more nearly realistic, ways. The Kantian school itself sought in the philosophy of values to adjust itself to the living consciousness of contemporary culture and, as in the later Natorp, it broke through the critical limits in philosophy of history. It began to become aware of the fact that there were metaphysical elements in its own presuppositions (Nikolai Hartmann) and such concepts as myth and symbol, for which there was no room in genuine Kantianism, gained fundamental philosophical importance (Cassirer). The crisis in critical, bourgeois philosophy was tragically regarded as a crisis in culture itself (Liebert). A survey of the rapidly growing Kant Society demonstrates not only the surprisingly rapid increase of philosophical interest but also the disappearance of original Kantianism from the castles of its former dominion.

Phenomenology came to be of decisive importance for the philosophy of the twentieth century. It arose, as we have previously indicated, out of Husserl's *Logical Studies* which appeared at the turn of the century and which represented a real turn in the philosophical movement. What phenomenology effected above all was a change in the intellectual point of view.

Instead of dissolving objects by means of critical analysis and of raising the question whether and how such objects exist, the essence of the things themselves is regarded quite apart from the question of their existence. The external, natural existence of things loses its domination over mind while the inner, spiritual essence, the ideal reality of things, is sought. In their totality the essences so apprehended present a world of ideas which transcends spatial and temporal reality and constitutes its truth. The apprehension of this world of essences is naturally impossible by way of critical reflection. Only devoted surrender to them and intuition can attain this end. External, natural and historical objects are only exemplars which must be used in apprehending essences. Not these things themselves in their existence but the essences in which they participate are to be known. The question of the *that,* the question of existence, may be raised only after the question about the *what* has been answered by means of phenomenological intuition.—The religious meaning of this change lies in the substitution of an attitude of surrender, of contemplation of the spiritual essence of things in their immediate givenness and meaning, for the dominating, bourgeois attitude which tears things to pieces and then seeks to reconstruct them. At the same time the recognition of a world of essence and truth which lies beyond the stream of time is of decisive importance for the destruction of the self-sufficient attitude of finite existence. With the rise of phenomenology a mystical element has entered into modern philosophy. Its entrance is not fortuitous for a clear line of relationship leads back from Husserl through Brentano and Bolzano to medieval philosophy and unites contemporary philosophy with the finest spirit of the Catholic tradition. It is therefore also not due to chance that phenomenology is exercising especially strong influences on circles influenced by Catholicism.

In connection with this development, it is necessary to give attention to a philosophical method which is closely related to the philosophy of life but is nevertheless quite distinct— the pragmatic method. Although it was most brilliantly formulated in Germany in Nietzsche's *Will to Power* and in Vaihinger's *Philosophy As If,* it attained actual leadership only in American philosophy. Renouncing the claim to truth-in-itself pragmatism declares those concepts or fictions to be true which are necessary to and which promote life. It cannot be established that they possess any other truth value in addition to this value for life. The philosophy is an almost picturesque expression of that attitude of domination over things which prevails in capitalist society, but it is neither critical nor rationalistic. Consequently this philosophy was able to yield highly conservative results when it dealt with religion, as in the case of William James's philosophy of religion. For from this point of view positive, confessional religion must be valued as a source of great power and therefore as pragmatically true. To be sure, these ideas show how very great is the difference between the American and the continental European situations. They indicate the pre-critical but also the fundamentally pre-spiritual character of the American mind. It is impossible to speak in this instance of a revolution in thought such as is apparent especially in Central Europe. Both the negative and the positive presuppositions of such a revolution are lacking.[1]

By contrast the way in which the European mind has turned to a new apprehension of spirit and the eternal becomes the more clearly apparent. That this change is taking place in phi-

---

[1] It is rather unfortunate that Tillich does not, at this point and a few others where he refers to men and movements in other countries than Germany, remain conscious of those limitations of all serious discussion of which he speaks in the Preface and the Introduction. James can scarcely be accused of that hyper-pragmatism which the author describes nor can he be made responsible for the conservative and reactionary uses to which his philosophy of religion has been put by the apologists for various orthodoxies.—*Translator.*

losophy, within the same sphere in which the rejection of the spiritual and the eternal occurred, is one of the most important symptoms of the present religious situation.

TWO

METAPHYSICS

The philosophic movement of the day is working out its destiny in a sphere which though closely related to science is yet independent of it, in metaphysics. To state the idea conversely and more accurately, the change in scientific attitude is a result of a change in metaphysical attitude. The metaphysical attitude of capitalist society is the rejection of metaphysics. Even such a rejection is metaphysical for it rests on faith in the self-sufficiency of the world and its forms. One refrains from saying this explicitly; one prefers to disguise it by means of epistemological discussions about the limits of knowledge.

It was quite in accordance with the facts, therefore, that the new movements in metaphysics directed attention first of all to the tacit pre-

79

suppositions which formed the basis of the old attack on metaphysics and cast doubt on their validity. The inadequacy of the solutions of the problem of reality which had been offered by critical idealism and by dogmatic materialism as well as insight into the original unity of the form and content of knowledge led to new approaches to the ontological problem. The old metaphysical question about the relation of essence and existence was raised anew by the phenomenological doctrine of essences. The philosophy of religion demanded particularly that the transcendental character of being and obligation be recognized. Despite all critical counterattacks these questions could not be silenced. Up to the present, it is true, philosophy is by no means clear about the real character of metaphysical cognition. That such knowledge does not belong to the system of scientific knowledge is scarcely doubted anywhere. But its relation to philosophy is obscure. Critical considerations inherited from the past period are still effective enough to delimit philosophy in the narrower sense from metaphysics. The relation is probably most correctly conceived in the description of metaphysics as an independent, essentially religious attitude of direction toward the Unconditioned; as such it makes use of scientific concepts in order to express symbolically that element of transcendence which is effective in and which supports knowledge. But the relation is in need of further clarification.

It may be noted that at the present time the metaphysics of being is less highly developed than is the metaphysics of history. The fact is not due to chance. Medieval metaphysics was a metaphysics of being because it arose out of the soil of static, non-historical mysticism. In the Protestant world the dynamic, moving spirit of historical reality has come to prevail in an increasing degree. The meaning of history seems more important to the mind than does the meaning of being. The metaphysical interpretation of the meaning of history has become an urgent and practical concern. The necessity of acting historically in the true sense, that is of acting so as to change history, is one of the strongest motives for the development of a metaphysics of history. One of its constantly effective forms is that utopian metaphysics which socialism derived from Hegel via Marx. It has become the occasion for the development of historico-metaphysical ideas of the sort which Ernst Troeltsch outlined in his *Historism and Its Problems,* for though his thought is more closely related to the capitalist metaphysics of progress yet he was also strongly influenced by romantic socialism. The metaphysics of progress which prevailed in capitalist society was attacked from another side by the organic and conservative interpretation of history which is related to German romanticism and which has been strangely developed by Spengler into a biological and aristocratic theory of history. Finally, notice must be taken of the energetic attempt made by the religious socialist movement to work out a metaphysics of history. In view of all that has been said there can be no doubt of the fact that we are standing in the very midst of intensive labor on the metaphysics of history. On this side the specious banishment of metaphysics has long been revoked. The bourgeois faith in progress was so evidently itself a metaphysics that with the growth of opposition to capitalist society a different interpretation of history was bound to arise. The closed circle of finite existence which is represented by the faith in progress has been broken; the presence of the eternal in time and history has been recognized. That this has happened so generally and emphatically is extremely important for the religious situation of the present.

The metaphysics of history naturally reacts on the metaphysics of being. The inner relationship of these two aspects of metaphysical thought constitutes a problem in itself. The recognition of the necessity of a metaphysical interpretation of history leads to the recognition of the necessity of metaphysics *per se.* But necessity is not actuality. This statement applies to all attempts to reach the goal too hastily, whether they are made in connection with idealism and romanticism or independently. Against such attempts the spirit of critical philosophy is still active; above all else it prevents the treatment of metaphysics as a demonstrable science, that is, as the grounding of the Unconditioned on the conditioned with the consequent destruction of the former. But it does not prevent thought from seeking the way to metaphysics itself, that is, by way of the intuition of the Unconditioned in the symbols of the conditioned. It no longer confines the spirit within the limits of self-contained finitude. In opposition to romanticism the new metaphysics must be realistic, in opposition to critical philosophy it must be a *belief-ful realism.*[1] No individual can fulfill the task of setting forth such a metaphysics. It is the task of a whole time and it will be the symbol in which a time will be able to see itself and its situation in the presence of eternity.

[1] For a discussion of the term *belief-ful realism* see the translator's introduction.—*Translator.*

THREE

ART

I. *Painting, Sculpture, Architecture and the Dance.* While science and philosophy have an immediate and causal significance for the spiritual situation of a time, whether as destructive or constructive forces, art is to be evaluated only as a mediate cause. For its immediate task is not that of apprehending essence but that of expressing meaning. Art indicates what the character of a spiritual situation is; it does this more immediately and directly than do science and philosophy for it is less burdened by objective considerations. Its symbols have something of a revelatory character while scientific conceptualization must suppress the symbolical in favor of objective adequacy. Science is of greater importance in the rise of a spiritual situation but art is the more important for its apprehension. In metaphysics the two interests are evenly balanced. It combines the will to apprehend objectively with the symbolic character of its conceptions.

The revolt against the spirit of capitalist society has been least ambiguously expressed in painting since the beginning of the century. The tendency which we have been accustomed to call expressionism, but which far transcends the narrower meaning of that term, is particularly symptomatic of that fact.—Bourgeois France was the unchallenged leader in painting during the nineteenth century. In reaction against idealism and romanticism and as a genuine product of the capitalist temper the naturalistic and impressionistic tendency developed extraordinary creative and formative power since the middle of the century. But its forms are the perfect forms of self-sufficient finitude, in naturalism on the side of the object, in impressionism more on the side of the subject. Reality as it is apprehended in the interaction between a natural subject and a natural object, the temporal moment, the impression is captured. And this is done with the creative power of genius, therefore magnificently and with the force of symbolism. But nowhere does one break through to the eternal, to the unconditioned content of reality which lies beyond the antithesis of subject and object. An undertone of quiet, naturalistic metaphysics accompanies everything, it is true, but it is the metaphysics of a finitude which postulates its own absoluteness.

With a will to create objectively, Cézanne battled with the form and restored to things their real metaphysical meaning. With passionate force van Gogh revealed the creative dynamic in light and color and the Scandinavian Munch showed the cosmic dread present in nature and mankind. Upon this basis new forces developed everywhere, in Italy, in France, in Germany and in Russia. Expressionism proper arose with a revolutionary consciousness and revolutionary force. The individual forms of things were dissolved, not in favor of subjective impressions but in favor of objective metaphysical expression. The abyss of Being was to be evoked in lines, colors and plastic forms. In Germany the painters of the "Bridge Circle," Schmidt-Rottluff, Nolde, Kirchner and Heckel, led the way. Others accompanied them. Naturally the movement turned back to older, primitive and exotic forms in which the inner expressive force of reality was still to be found untamed. The discovery of primitive and Asiatic art came to be the symbol of revolt against the spirit of capitalist society.—One peculiar movement followed the general tendency under the catchword titles of futurism, cubism and constructivism. The dissolution of the natural forms of things took on geometric character. Therein the feeling was expressed that every picturization of organic forms under the rule of the capitalist, rationalist spirit was insincere. At the same time the planes, lines and cubes which were used received an almost mystical transparency. In this case as in expressionism in general the self-sufficient form of existence was broken through. Not a transcendent world is depicted as in the art of the ancients but the transcendental reference in things to that which lies beyond them is expressed.

This distinction appears very clearly in the religious art of the period. Even naturalistic painting had used the old religious symbols of art; the figure of Jesus above all played a certain rôle. But the manner of representation was clearly analogous to the liberal conception of Jesus which prevailed in the Protestant theology of the period, so that at best an ideal, finite reality but never the reference to the eternal was expressed. The religious art of capitalist society reduces the traditional religious symbols to the level of middle-class morality and robs them of their transcendence and their sacramental character. Expressionism, on the contrary, has a mystical, religious character, quite apart from

its choice of subjects. It is not an exaggeration
to ascribe more of the quality of sacredness to a
still-life by Cézanne or a tree by van Gogh than
to a picture of Jesus by Uhde. But as soon as expressionism itself turns to religious subjects its
characteristic limitations are revealed. Its mysticism stands outside the religious tradition. It
cannot derive inspiration from the old symbols
nor can it find a new meaning in them. When
it attempts to do so it becomes either a faint
echo out of the past, as in the case of Eberz with
his Catholic background, or it transforms the
symbols and substitutes human devotion for the
divine deed, as, perhaps, in Schmidt-Rottluff,
Nolde and Heckel. This process is highly characteristic of the contemporary religious situation. It indicates how the continuity of the religious tradition has been broken by capitalist
culture and how the modern religious consciousness must find itself again, without the aid of
any definite symbolism, in a pure, mystic immediacy. But this may be done by means of any
symbol.

The method which is employed by this spiritual interpretation of reality begins with the
breaking up of its natural forms, of its immediate existential character, of its self-contained
finitude. The third dimension and perspective
—these forms which seem to confer independent

existence on things—are negated in particular. It is quite understandable why all those who do not recognize spirit or who wish to have it at best as an idealization of finite existence, but always without a break with that existence, should protest passionately against this art. But the very vehemence of this protest on the part of capitalist society shows that a vital attack has been made upon its spirit.

The extent to which this protest was historically justified became apparent in the movements of the last few years which are of sufficient significance for the religious situation of our time to deserve the closest attention. A realism has suddenly appeared in art which, in George Gross and Otto Dix, verges on caricature in its vindictive opposition to the bourgeois culture that revealed its character in the world war. It was a brutal realism which though it rejected all the romantic elements of expressionism yet had no relation to the realism of the previous period. The tendency to caricature gradually ceased and forms were developed which one may possibly speak of as the beginnings of a *belief-ful realism*. The movement has frequently been regarded simply as an antithesis to expressionism so that the bourgeois spirit believed itself on the way to a new triumph. But in truth a mighty antagonist to that spirit has appeared; it is carrying the battle into the very camp of the enemy and employing his own best weapons against him. There is grave danger, of course, that this enterprise will be defeated by the overpowering force of the capitalist spirit. It is true of this battle also that the warfare is difficult and full of retreats and round-about ways to victory.

We have discussed painting so extensively because it is particularly fruitful and revelatory for our problem. Sculpture followed analogous lines while architecture made use of expressionistic forms only rarely and then with evident lack of success. For its relation to the practical end of construction forces a realism upon it from which the free arts with their non-utilitarian character can readily emancipate themselves. Hence architecture achieved its real successes in the service of that most realistic of modern ends, the economic end, in the construction of railroad stations, factories, commercial and office buildings, as, for instance, the Chile House in Hamburg. Yet it is a spiritualized realism which speaks out of these things. They point toward a transcendent reference in technique and economic life, toward the growth of a mythical interpretation of these functions which had been evaluated in purely rationalist and imperial terms in the capitalist period. At all events it is highly characteristic of the religious situation of the present that it is not religious buildings but economic structures which reveal a little of this tendency toward self-transcendence, of the will to break through the limits of self-sufficient finitude. Religious architecture on the other hand is like religious painting; it is without symbolic power to express the religious situation of the present.

From the point of view of our problem the art of the dance has a value all of its own. It is significant, to begin with, that this art has experienced a complete renaissance during the last quarter of a century and is recognized again as an independent form of spiritual expression. In an increasing degree it has developed away from its individualistic, estheticizing beginnings in a direction which leads toward what one may possibly identify as the ritual dance. To be sure a less hospitable soil for such a development than the soil of the Christian, specifically of the Protestant, West can scarcely be imagined. Under such circumstances achievements such as those of the Laban school and particularly those of Mary Wigman are all the more significant. Their group-dances indicate the defeat of individualism; the figures of the dance seek to give inner content and organization to space, the expressive gestures try to reveal metaphysical meanings. All of this is still in its beginnings and the movement would be gravely imperiled should it seek on its own initiative to create a ritual in the narrower sense of that term.

The last statement applies to the whole sphere of creative art. It can express metaphysical meanings; it cannot produce them. The inadequacy of all false romanticism—in art, science and social theory—appears in its effort to derive an absolute content from the form, that is to say, it tries to capture and preserve eternity by means of a movement in time. In contrast to such attempts the spirit of capitalist society which seeks to hold fast to the finite as something finite is more honest and therefore stronger. Eternity is first of all the "no" which is uttered against time, the shaking of the present, and only insofar as it is that can temporal forms point toward the eternal.

II. *Literature.* It is exceedingly difficult to discover in the tremendous wealth of European literature in all its types a clear line of development corresponding to our approach to our problem. It is even less possible to do this in this sphere than it is in art. Subjective bias in evaluation as well as in selection is unavoidable. Yet the influence of literature on the religious situation of a period, by virtue of the superiority of words over lines and colors, is both more direct and more general than is the influence of art. Hence we must at least make the attempt to discover in literature also the expression of the revolt against capitalist society and to inquire into its significance for the whole social consciousness.

Emile Zola was at one and the same time the friend of the impressionist circle and the most potent representative of naturalism. The spirit of scientific, rationalistic observation dominates his style completely; the scientific attitude threatens constantly to overpower the literary attitude. Content corresponds to attitude; it is critical naturalism. The self-sufficient finitude of bourgeois society is criticized with tremendous passion but the standard of criticism is that finitude itself and its ideal form as it is to be achieved under the leadership of science. There is no trace of an inner self-transcendence. This is also true by and large of Ibsen's dramatic works. In content they are a criticism of bourgeois society and of the hypocrisy of its conventions but the standards employed are those of the society itself. Yet he does transcend these limitations at certain points, as in *Peer Gynt*, for instance. Similarly Flaubert's naturalism does not prevent him from assimilating some mystic elements in the course of his development. The influence of a Catholicizing mysticism, though in a negative and demonic form, is unambiguously present in Baudelaire's lyrics of decadence. But this element is not strong enough to bring emancipation from the bondage to the capitalist spirit. The contradiction is present but it remains dependent on that which is contradicted. It is the expression of the isolation of the culturally over-refined individual who has lost his social character and substance, the expression of his despair in his loneliness and impoverishment.

Decisive impulses toward change were given by Strindberg who moved on the one hand in the negative realm of the bourgeois period but went beyond it on the other hand both in the form and content of his work. The figures in his drama take on a typical form; they are removed beyond the accidents of existence and impression. The transcendent sphere enters into the action. The figures become symbolic and transparent; the boundaries of reality become vague. Monastic asceticism and mysticism appear to be the goal of the development. In Germany a similar tendency appears in Gerhart Hauptmann as well as in other European dramatists. These tendencies are even more noticeable in the novel. The high regard in which the work of E. T. A. Hoffmann is held is characteristic. Directly mystical and theosophical subject matter is preferred and this begins to loosen up the fixed conception of reality established by the natural sciences. In lyric poetry Hugo von Hoffmannsthal and Dehmel did not, to be sure, break through the circle of the purely immanent but in their language they did call up real emotions which were not merely subjective impressions but developed into metaphysical meanings. This movement was accompanied by the impressionistic tendency in literature which was most perfectly represented, so far as its form is concerned, by Thomas Mann and which achieved in him, as painting did in the later work of Clovis Corinth, a distinction transcending the subjectivism and estheticism of the attitude as a whole.

In Rilke poetry is given a directly religious turn. In his mysticism there is an echo of the impressionistic tendency to dissolve all nature into the feelings and contemplations of the subject. But what is really contemplated and felt is the religious content in the sense of neo-Platonic and medieval tradition. The religious influence which these poems exercised is not to be underestimated even though their strong estheticism is taken into calculation. They prepared the way for movements which could go farther. By far the most important poet of the time is Stefan George. His union of the classic with the Catholic spirit in a highly disciplined style was one of the most powerful protests against the spirit of capitalist society with its reduction of all things to a common level, a common shallowness and spiritual impoverishment. The discipline and difficulty of his diction, his earnest, ascetic efforts to find the right, symbolic word, his fundamental, metaphysical view of life and reality, his determination to find the pure form which is superior to subject and object—all this gave an impulse which led to further consequences in the philosophy of art and spirit. There is one limitation indeed which George shares with capitalist society—the lack of a comprehensive, community-forming religious content. His aristocratic exclusiveness is conditioned by the classical element which is present in him and at that point he is in contact with the capitalist society which also derives from humanism and classicism. The sphere of the finite forms is not really transcended. The classic form not only tames chaos but also bars the way to the invasion which proceeds from the Unconditioned and which therefore breaks through every form. The creative *Eros,* in George's movement, is communicated by individual to individual, hence it remains limited to small circles and is expressed in spiritual but not in universal terms. George is not the "Lord of the Era," that is, the symbol and conqueror of our present time, as his disciples would have him be. He lacks the universality and the extra-verted force of prophetic personality which are necessary for that rôle. He is a fountain of priestly spirit for many but not of the prophetic spirit for all.

The major line of literary development did not grow so much out of the synthetic and highly formal tendencies which George repre-sents as out of the destructive tendencies which announced their appearance in Dehmel and be-came victorious, thanks largely to the powerful influence of Nietzsche, in the last pre-war gen-eration. Nietzsche's battle against the hypocrisy of bourgeois convention led to a dynamic up-rush of those primal forces, the will-to-power and the erotic drive. It was all still saturated, to be sure, with naturalistic influences, but con-tained a demonic transcendence, nevertheless, which was absolutely repulsive to the capitalist spirit. Such phenomena as Kasimir Edschmid and Heinrich Mann are typical as is Wedekind in the sphere of the drama and as are a number of lyric poets. Franz Werfel, who is akin to these in style but wholly opposed to them in his tend-ency, goes on his own, independent way. He substitutes humility, love of the lowliest, the ac-ceptance of fate, for the will to power and the erotic drive. Things are seen as united in a profound, all-controlling community of suffering and love; even the vulgar and the loathsome are not excluded. The hard surfaces and the resistances in things are erased. Things are robbed of their objectivity without being dissolved into nothingness. This strange softness is expressed even in the language and in its dissolving character, in strong contrast to Stefan George.

It is in place to call attention at this point to the rediscovery of Dostoievski and to the religious significance of this event. What is religiously effective in this is the mystical realism of the Russian novelist, his contemplation of the demonic and negative elements in actuality on the basis of a present divine reality. Even in the most extreme antitheses to bourgeois morality this divine element is not lacking; in fact it is more readily discovered there than in bourgeois society. Thanks to the tremendous greatness of Dostoievski's characters it was not clearly perceived how alien they were to the Western consciousness and their spirit was effective even where there was no inkling of the thoroughness of the antithesis. Their effect was, in consequence, frequently only esthetic and therefore passing.

War and revolution influenced literature in this wise, that the catastrophe of capitalist civilization in the world war was regarded with revolutionary emotions and expressed in revolutionary form. It is highly significant for our situation that no literature affirming and glorifying war was produced; the slight attempts which were made in this direction were marked by such a heavy realism that one would prefer to classify them with the negative reactions. The war was experienced everywhere as a catastrophe of culture, as the unmasking of the demonic character of capitalist society. In literature as in painting the experience stimulated that super-realism which was dominated at first by social and political passions and then slowly achieved objectivity. Becher, Unruh, Toller and others used expressionistic forms to set forth these meanings. But in all of them the tendency is toward the demonic. They see the destructive demonic forces not in sex and the will-to-power, as was the case in the pre-war literature, but in the inescapable power of objective social institutions and movements. For this reason this literature is more profound, more despairing, more realistic. The romantic elements disappear. The conflict of the generations, the struggle of child with parent, which comes sharply to the fore in the most recent drama, combines the demonic forces of sex and society in peculiar fashion and indicates how completely the present has broken with the tradition of the capitalist spirit.

If we would characterize in summary fashion the religious situation of the present as it is presented in literature we should need to say that the realism and impressionism of the capitalist period have been destroyed in the development of symbolism, mysticism and expressionism but that a new realism is about to gain ascendancy; with emotional zeal at first, then with objective and metaphysical intuition it has uncovered the demonism present in the social world and, perhaps, as in the case of metaphysics and painting, it may be at the point of developing into **a** *belief-ful realism.*

Part Two

THE PRESENT RELIGIOUS SITUATION
IN POLITICS AND ETHICS

ONE

THE POLITICAL SPHERE

I. *Economics and Sociology.* The spirit of a
finitude which lives within itself is, for our
time, the spirit of capitalist society. The desig-
nation itself indicates that the primary place
where this spirit realizes itself is the sphere of
activity. Within this sphere, however, it is economic activity which is dominant and it is its
unconditioned dominance which characterizes
the capitalist spirit most definitely. Economic
activity as such is not the expression of self-
sufficient finitude, but economic activity as occu-
pying a certain position in the social whole and
the consequent ways in which it carries on its
activity constitute this expression.

Capitalist society took its rise with the emancipation of economic activity from control by a
superior social power and the development of

an autonomous economic system subject only to its own laws. Classical economics is the theoretic apprehension of the laws of such an independent economic activity, the science of its rational principles, abstracted from relation to the total social organism. The free market, the regulation of production by supply and demand, the unlimited possibilities of making profits and accumulating capital, these are all things in which autonomous economic activity realizes itself. They correspond to the rationalistic methods of natural science and lead to the same results in the relations between things and in social relations. In the free market economy the attitude toward material things comes to be dominating, loveless, without the sense of community with them. Things become wares—objects whose meaning lies in the production of profits in transactions of buying and selling, not in the enrichment of the personal life. They are acquired and disposed of by their masters, not by beings who have some kind of community with them. Hence there is no limit to their acquisition. Free economy tends necessarily toward infinite commercial imperialism. It is infinite but only in the sphere of the finite. Just because it is infinite it is the most complete expression of a finitude which is sufficient to itself, which is ever restless but which never transcends itself.

In the past man's relation to material things was hallowed by reverence and awe, by piety toward and gratitude for his possessions. In the pre-capitalist era there was something transcendent in man's relation to things. The thing, property, was a symbol of participation in a God-given world, proportionate to one's position according to which one had a larger or smaller share in the world. The ware, on the other hand, is a symbol of the infinite finitude of the pure desire to exercise rulership. Consequently the limited possessions such as land, house, cattle, furniture, clothing, etc., lose their symbolic meaning. They become utility wares, conditioned wholly by their utility in the service of consumption—produced, treated and given away without love or a sense of their individuality. They receive not only the meaning but also the actual form of wares. This dominating, loveless attitude toward things has a twofold religious effect. It emancipates men from finite holy things which claim for themselves the holiness of the eternal; it releases them from a sanctified bondage to things and exalts personality above the whole realm of things. That is the protestant effect of liberal economy. At the same time, however, it confines personality by pressing it into endless service in the rule over impoverished things; thus personality itself is impoverished and devoted to the world of the finite. That is the effect of the capitalist spirit in liberal economy.

The illimitable need for things and the ability which is given the merchant of awakening illimitable wants correspond to the lovelessness of our relationship to things. Love and piety are directed toward limited possessions, whose content and meaningful form satisfy the spirit. Things which have lost their meaning do not satisfy; they drive men on from one thing to another and there is no possibility of satisfaction. Impoverished personality is left without a definitely directed love. It is open to every allurement brought to it from without. That is the reason why the possibility of arousing wants through salesmanship and advertising is unlimited. In this also there is a religious element, positive in its significance. It is the emancipation of man from an earthbound, unambitious dullness; it is the civilizing release of personality from the bonds of animal existence and from the merely fortuitous satisfaction of its needs. At the same time, however, this emancipation implies coercion to engage in unending, ever-increasing, life-consuming activity in the service of unlimited wants. It means the domination of the economic function over all the other functions of life; its consequence is bondage to time and hence also the lack of time for attention to the eternal. This is one of the weightiest characteristics of the capitalist time. The goad of unlimited desire does not allow the spirit time for anything which does not serve time itself. It drives the spirit about within the inescapable and unending circle of the finite.

The influence of liberal economy on social relationships was even more important than its destruction of the old attitude of love of things. The free market is the manifestation of the conflict of interests, of the war of all against all, accepted as a principle, hence of an activity motivated always by the impulse to seek one's own interests at the expense of others. The peculiarly demonic element in the situation of capitalist society is this, that the conflict is not the expression of individual arbitrariness or of chaotic anarchy but is necessarily bound up with the maintenance of the capitalist economic system and is the result of that system itself. But the universal conflict of interests becomes effective in the large only when it is combined with a relative balance of inclusive group-interests, that is to say, with the principle of solidarity. The most important conflict which results in this fashion from the liberal economy is the conflict between the owners of the means of production and those who are dependent on these

means but do not own them, the conflict between capitalists and wage-workers. It is true
that this antagonism does not cancel the antago-
nisms within the groups themselves. Solidarity
is always provisional and tactical; it is always
based on a merely partial, never on a complete,
identification of interests. Consequently it can
be dissolved at any time and it is able to form a
real community only when it is combined with
other social forces.

The chief antithesis in capitalist society receives its profound and demonic character from
the fact that it develops into a class antithesis
and class conflict. Class contrasts are the contrasts of the various fates of men; class is inclusive of all aspects of the spiritual and social life,
even though the economic aspect is fundamental. The formation of classes means that a radical rupture has taken place in the human community and that its solidarity before the eternal
has been radically destroyed. The component
elements of the self-sufficient finite world regard
themselves as absolute, each in its own right,
instead of seeing themselves as complementary
pointers toward the eternal.

The fateful result of this whole situation is
that men, particularly the masses, are impoverished spiritually for the sake of their service to
the machine, that the mechanical production of

the human mass takes place. For the mass is formed by soldering together atomized individuals which have lost all individual quality. Mass is the social form of that part of society which is bound by natural law only, which has been robbed of its vital meaning and which has been made subject to finite ends alone. The mechanized mass and its instinctive movements are the terrible, destructive by-products of the demonic element in the capitalist spirit. The capitalist class which stands in antithesis to the mass has the means of education at its disposal, to be sure, but it uses them partly for the sake of exercising efficient control over nature and the mass and partly for the sake of achieving individual self-realization without the sense of a metaphysical responsibility for self and society. Spirit in the service of a rational management of things and an irresponsible spirit—these are the two consequences of the fact that capitalist society has sundered the reference of the spirit to the eternal.

Our problem required the careful consideration of these things because they determine the religious situation of the present more than almost anything else and because, up to the present time, the counter movements have not succeeded in removing the fateful results of this situation. This applies first and above all to socialism, the greatest and most effective of the movements in opposition to capitalist society. Almost all the weapons which can be used in the war against capitalist society were forged in the socialist critique which developed throughout the whole nineteenth century and which achieved its climax in Marx's and Engels' *Communist Manifesto* with its sweeping and prophetic power. Now if the spirit of capitalist society is the spirit of self-sufficient finitude then opposition to this spirit should imply a breaking through the circle of the finite. It cannot in fact be denied and it has long been recognized that there is a transcendent element, something which goes beyond the sphere of finite possibilities, in the passionate, eschatological tension, in the dynamic hopefulness of the original socialist movement. In the ultimate bases of socialism there was an element of religious eschatology. It was a great victory of the capitalist spirit, however, perhaps the greatest victory that it has won, when it took captive the strongest of the movements directed against it. The ultimately transcendent goal of socialism was made finite and temporal in its actual definition of ends. It looked forward to a point in time when that which is the negation of all time—the eternal— was to be realized. The necessary result of this inner contradiction was that socialism should become disillusioned, should begin to make compromises, to adopt the doctrine of progress and to become bourgeois in its temper. Even the extreme movements which, like communism, resist this tendency contain a sufficiently strong element of the capitalist spirit to fall victim to this illusion again and again. The attitude is partly due to the fact that socialism has had to fight not only for the conquest of capitalist society but also for the vital interests of a proletariat which exists in the midst of that society. But the two purposes are tragically opposed to each other. At the same time socialism accepted the theoretical and practical thought-patterns of the capitalist period and so occupied fundamentally the same position as did its opponent. Thorough-going as is the antagonism of the socialist masses to the fate which capitalist society has brought upon them they are nevertheless incapable of escaping the influences with which that society encircles them and of breaking through the system of self-sufficient finitude.

Along with the general revolt against the temper of capitalist society a change in socialist thought took place. The extent to which the actual socialist movement had fallen prey to the spirit of the nineteenth century was recognized and new goals were projected which lay beyond the sphere which capitalist and socialist thought occupied in common. Landauer's *Call to Social-ism,* a typical reaction from Marxist to romantic socialism, belongs to this movement. The communism of Lukacs and others is less romantic and closer to Marx but it interprets the latter more from the Hegelian than from the Kantian or the materialistic point of view. Syndicalism with its notable French theorists and such ideas as those which Kropotkin and Bakunin represented in Russia emphatically opposed the capitalist tendency toward centralization and the thorough-going, unitary rationalization of the whole world, which state socialism also approached. Disturbing elements have also entered the party from the youth movement via the young socialists. Beginning with the ultimate religious presuppositions religious socialism, as represented particularly by the Berlin group gathered about Mennicke, grapples with these problems. All of these movements seek to interpret socialism as a part of a comprehensive spiritual movement, to make it an organic part of the whole anti-capitalist attitude and to eliminate all capitalistic elements from it. They reject the naïve sense of absoluteness of the socialist party, as expressed both by leaders and the masses. They struggle for a new definition of the theoretical basis and the practical end of the movement. Hence they deal with the problems of community, of the attitude toward things, with the questions about human needs, about the formation of classes, with the problem of the masses in its economic and religious aspects, with the problem of property, the meaning of the liberal definition of the economic laws and with other similar questions. Their criticism of socialism is often radical, more radical and profound, indeed, than that which is exercised by capitalism; yet it is a criticism which is at the same time an affirmation of the socialist struggle.

It was inevitable that romantic elements, in comparison with which the old movement possesses superior justification, should enter into these tendencies. The period of the revolution particularly, with its eager anticipations, promoted an unrealistic enthusiasm which could not long endure. The actual power of the controlling capitalism and the superior strength of the bourgeois, rationalist temper which influenced all aspects of life were far too great to be set aside by a revolution, even by a successful one. Actual attempts to anticipate the realization of the socialist ideal in the organization of small communities, settlements, etc., failed unless they adjusted themselves to the general economic system. So the older generation of socialist leaders continues to hold fast to the bourgeois, rationalist elements in its tradition while young socialism remains without influence for the present. Religious socialism is shaken by the doubt which arises out of the question which is most fundamental and most difficult for it, How is it possible from the standpoint of religion or the eternal to reach any decisions which are applicable to the world of time? Under the pressure of this question it is being almost visibly de-romanticized. It above all others raises the demand for that which we have designated *belief-ful realism,* that is an unconditioned acceptance of the serious importance of our concrete situation in time and of the situation of time in general in the presence of eternity; such an attitude contains the negation of every kind of romanticism and utopianism but it includes the hope of a social and economic life in which the spirit of capitalism—the symbol of self-sufficient finitude—has been overcome. It is impossible to predict to what extent the bourgeois and the sometimes even more resistant socialist groups can be imbued with this consciousness or what its consequences for the organization of economic life and for the political struggle will be. Only this is certain, that the social and economic order of capitalism, even on the side of orthodox socialism, has been shaken to its foundations and that the tremors can no more be quieted.

II. *Nation and Mankind.* Capitalist society is in principle cosmopolitan society, for the rationalistic elimination of all qualities includes the elimination of the specific qualities of the nations and their subordination of a uniform humanity. It is noteworthy that the development and actual form of capitalist society contradicted this logical consequence of its principle from the very beginning. The democratic idea was represented by England and France, that is, by nations which by virtue of that idea had arrived at national self-consciousness before all others. The idea was given an abstract, cosmopolitan formulation primarily there where no such national reality supported it, as in German philosophy. The democratic nations on the other hand found their historic mission in the promotion of the spirit of capitalist society. Their national self-consciousness was rooted in a religious sense of destiny. National sovereignty was for them the realization of divine, that is to say, democratic sovereignty. This consciousness in a strongly secularized form still supports the great western democracies. This corresponds to what we said at the beginning of the religious sources of bourgeois society. The sense of national destiny, however, contains also the idea that the other nations are to be subjected to it. It is essentially universalistic and imperialistic.

This element in the national self-consciousness comes into antagonism with its real democratic content and the antithesis is necessarily called hypocrisy by those who do not understand the situation. But it is not hypocrisy and it is not true that English and American democracies, for instance, use humanitarian principles only for the purpose of extending national power without believing in them; the sense of national vocation is really present and represents the indissoluble unity of religious faith and national will-to-power.

It was inevitable that in their resistance to this imperialistic nationalism national self-consciousness should also develop on the part of the threatened peoples. Out of this development arose the mystic sense of nationalism which is so strong a reaction against the capitalist spirit. It believed that organic ideas were to take the place of rationalistic and atomistic concepts. The nation was to regard itself as a community in its inner relations, as a significant, individual being in its external relations; the various vocational groups were to stand in a relation of mutual responsibility to each other and to the whole community; the whole, however, was to be filled with a meaning which has its source and goal in the eternal. To be sure this conservative Christian nationalism did not see that in international relations it left individualism and the liberal conflict of interests quite untouched. For this view never attains to the ideal of an inclusive human community like the medieval ideal of a united Christendom.

The old conservative national position has been forced back by capitalist society, though only step by step. Party victories within the nation which were won only by slow stages were much less important in that process than were the situation and attitude in foreign relations and the alliance between conservatives and liberals which was conditioned by that attitude. In this situation the liberal element present in the conservative position was revealed. The theory of national liberalism explicitly contains the combination of the principle of nationalism with the spirit of capitalist society. In essence it contains the demand for internal rule by capital and for the external extension of capitalist power. Through the victory of national liberalism over conservatism the principle of nationality was subordinated to the spirit of capitalist society.

This combination, however, contains an inner contradiction the unresolvability of which leads to extremely serious consequences. In its inner structure capitalist society stands in complete antithesis to the principle of nationalism. The

organization of the people in the interest of economic efficiency destroys the organic structure
by vocations and leads to the division into
classes; the efficient economic organization of
the world destroys national individuality and
imposes the capitalistic pattern on all nations.
In the face of this development the original idea
of vocation can as little maintain itself as can the
mystic and organic conception of the national
spirit. If the principle of nationality is maintained nevertheless it now receives the meaning
of an association for the promotion of common
interests in the world economic system with national armaments at its disposal for the sake of
economic expansion. The development discloses
the inner contradiction present in the whole
position. It becomes apparent as an actual contradiction voiced by the proletariat. It is true
that the proletariat can also derive profits from
national economic expansion but this does not
relieve it of its proletarian fate. And this fate
consists just in this, that mechanization and the
industrial formation of industrial masses have
led to the loss of a living relation to the soil, the
homeland, the native tongue, the common life
and the spirit of the nation. It is a testimony
for rather than against the national consciousness of the proletariat that it cannot feel its solidarity with a nation which has become an eco-

nomic association rather than an incorporation of the national spirit. Consequently the proletarian consciousness turns to the ideal of humanity without the mediation of nationality and the religious sense of mission is transferred from the nation to the whole human proletariat as a class. By its acceptance of the idea of humanity and of the pacifist ideal the proletariat has taken up one of the fundamental tendencies in capitalist society and has carried it through to its logical consequences. By relating this idea to the working class the proletariat proclaims its resolution to fight capitalist society. For this reason socialism tends to be pacifist only so far as international relations are concerned; where class relationships come into question it tends to be warlike and revolutionary.

Capitalist society also was forced to make concessions to the pacifist consequences of its fundamental principle. But because of its connection with nationalism it could not proceed otherwise than by seeking to build up an organization of mankind on the foundation of individual nationalities and by trying to find in the League of Nations a democratic safeguard by means of which disturbances of the world-embracing capitalist economy might be avoided. However strong may be the religious forces, the sense of the vocation of democractic nations, the humanitarian Utopianism which lie in the background of pacifism—particularly of American pacifism—the foreground is occupied by interest in the undisturbed functioning of the world-wide economic process and in the economic profit of individuals guaranteed by that process. It is the desire for a self-sufficient economic world which supports capitalist pacifism and, to a large extent, socialist pacifism also. Its original religious motives have been largely lost. An Anglo-American or a proletarian economic peace is regarded as the goal of the super-national development of humanity.

Religious socialism and similarly the patriotic Young Germans seek, partly in common enterprises, to emancipate the principle of nationalism from romantic and reactionary as well as from nationalistic and capitalistic elements. What success can attend such efforts on the hotly contested field of nationalism cannot be foreseen. At all events their success or failure will have considerable importance for the religious situation. For it is one of the most obscure of the demonic effects of the spirit of capitalist society that it has so thoroughly permeated and deformed the national principle which actually stands in decided antithesis to it.

III. *The State and the Constitution.* Among the ideas which betray the true character of capitalist society is its conception of the state. In the pre-capitalist period the state as the law-giving and law-enforcing community possessed the unction and sanctity which naturally belongs to it when the whole community regards it as the fundamental structure of the social life, determining all aspects of the social culture. Conflicts with the church in the medieval period were unable to deprive it of its sanctity. For these conflicts were possible only because two representatives of the universal spiritual and cultural life fought with each other, the state upon the secular, the church upon the sacred side; but the state could lay claim at the same time to the religious and the church to the secular side of life.

The capitalist conception of the state may be characterized as its complete secularization. With the disintegration of the communal life and of its spiritual and religious substance the only task which is still assigned to the state is the legal protection of the economic life in internal and external relations. The more efficiently it fulfills this task and the more quietly and securely the economic life can go on its way the truer the state is to its own nature. Interferences with the religious and spiritual sphere are out of the question for it. Its relation to religion and culture is defined by the idea of toleration; the violation of personality in its relation to the meaning of life, that is, in its faith, is eliminated, but at the same time the political community itself loses all significance for the ultimate meaning of life. The relationship of man to the eternal is removed from the political and public sphere and relegated to the private. The self-evident and logical consequence of making religion a private matter and the concern of private associations was drawn in Germany only by the Social Democrats. In England and America not only religion but a large part of the educational system also has been left to private control. To the extent to which this tendency increases the state naturally loses its original sancity and becomes a rather empty, technical machine with which the individual will concern himself as little as possible.

Such a machine, however, cannot run of its own accord. A purely legal pattern does not possess the power to make itself an actually existent body if it is not supported by actual living forces. The vital force which supported the capitalist state was nationalism. On the continent as well as in England and America it reendowed the state with a certain sanctity, gave it the ability to arouse enthusiasm, to demand sacrifices, even to interfere occasionally in the religious and spiritual sphere and to set rather definite limits to the principle of toleration. On this basis it was possible for the ideal of a Christian national state or even of a pagan national state to play a certain, fairly important, rôle in German thought. But the spirit of capitalist society was strong enough to prevent any serious threat to the principle of toleration or to the function of the state as the protector of the economic life.

In Germany it was socialism which first of all drew the logical consequences of the liberal theory of the state. Yet socialism never entertained this theory really seriously; what it truly desired was the development of a religious and spiritual culture on the basis of the socialist idea. Its demands that religion be made a purely private matter or that education be wholly secularized were after all only preliminary steps towards its real purpose which was to make socialist religion and culture fundamental in the public consciousness and in the various educational institutions. This was necessarily the case. For while in its tactics socialism has largely been the executor of liberal tendencies in Germany, it is really anti-liberal in nature. Its fundamental idea stands in contradiction to the secularism of capitalist political theory. It has been exceedingly unfortunate for the effectiveness of socialism, to be sure, that it has not produced its own theory of the state. It was prevented from doing this by the anarchistic elements present in its thought; despite the temporary acceptance of state socialism these elements remain in force so far as the definition of the final goal is concerned and they have been expressly reaffirmed by Lenin in dependence on Marx. The idea that with the elimination of the class conflict the state also must disappear and be replaced by local self-government represents the secular form of the ancient religious idea of the perfect community of love in the perfect Kingdom of God. Tolstoi has given the idea its most brilliant presentation. But Utopian socialism in the form given it by Landau or in the mystic form represented by the Zionist Martin Buber has not remained ineffective either and also belongs to the romantic revolt against the capitalist idea of the state. Religious socialism has been far more realistic in its attempt to work out the theory of the state and it stands in closer relation therefore to the representatives of the national idea. It seeks to develop a theory which will not only avoid the mistakes of capitalist, secular political rationalism but also those of romantic and nationalistic or anarchistic mysticism. In this case also romanticism is being transformed into a *belief-ful realism*.

The theory of the political constitution is

closely related to the theory of the state and it is also important for the interpretation of the religious situation, particularly in Germany where it has been the subject of bitter conflicts and of intensive thought. One effect of the spirit of capitalism was the elimination of that relationship of rulers and ruled which was the natural product of history and which had received a natural sanctity; it was replaced by the construction of a state out of atomic individuals who imposed a common legal obligation on themselves through the adoption of a social contract. In theory such a contract could lead even to princely absolutism, in fact it tended toward democracy. In and of itself democracy may have a mystical religious basis in the principle, "The voice of the people is the voice of God." But this original idea has long since disappeared and the formal principle of equality, made practically usable by means of majority rule, dominates democratic thinking. All reference to the eternal in the sense of a fate or a grace which supports the aristocracy or the ruler has been eliminated. Government is the rational business of politically talented persons. It is a profession, not a calling.

A democratic pattern of government, however, is quite as unreal as a purely formal state apparatus. The power which supports democracy is made up of the forces which can make use of it in establishing their own dominion in place of the sacred old aristocracies. The pillar of democracy is the middle class and particularly that part of the middle class which exercises economic leadership, in whose hands lies the control of capital. Middle class democracy is the political expression of capitalism. Capital creates majorities and with majorities it creates political power. When, for some reason or another, it cannot control a majority it deprives the state of power and indirectly, through its control of the economic sphere, makes the state dependent upon it.

Here again the peculiar situation appears that socialism, the antagonist of the capitalist spirit, in the very act of revolting against the domination of capital, carries the democratic idea through to its logical conclusion. Of course the polemical attitude of socialism has prevented it in this instance as in others from achieving an independent solution of the problem of state organization. Socialist theory has failed to recognize the actual power of certain groups and their very great importance in the government. The extreme groups with their doctrine of the dictatorship of the proletariat were the first to make an absolutely anti-democratic and anti-capitalistic demand, without possessing, how-

ever, the most essential means for realizing it.[1]

The conservative, nationalist opposition against the principle of a democratic constitution was more important because it was supported by stronger social forces. The principle of monarchy was relatively unimportant in this movement although it was espoused as the religiously sanctioned form of government. The actual strength of the conservative opposition was furnished rather by the idea of the organic state, by the conviction that the primal and natural relationship between rulers and ruled must be retained or reëstablished. The ideal of an organization by callings arose again and was endowed with a kind of mythical unction. This idea was combined with the principle of nationalism to form a Christian, conservative philosophy of society which became effective as a spiritual force in wide circles, particularly among youth, and which was even able to unite temporarily, in the form of a soviet system, with the revolutionary movement.

The romanticism of this conservative theory of a society organized by callings lies in the fact that it seeks to achieve by political action something which, according to its own conception even, must be the product of organic growth.

---

[1] Tillich is speaking, of course, about the German situation primarily.—*Translator*.

Such attempts are bound to fail and will always have the consequence that the actual powers, the supporters of capitalist control, will take the place which according to the organic theory should be occupied by the representatives of the community. Agrarian feudalism and capitalist feudalism unite and amalgamate and instead of achieving an organic structure of society succeed only in intensifying the class struggle. The organic, mystical theory of government is as little able to evade the influence of the spirit of capitalist society as is socialism. Self-sufficient finitude remains undisturbed. Forms of government which possess a transcendent sanctity, a social structure which contains an intrinsic and holy meaning cannot be discovered. Even the efforts of religious socialism to attain at least theoretical clarity in this field are only in their initial stages.

THE ETHICAL SPHERE

I. *Social Problems.* It has been a long time since a movement has received so much attention as has been accorded to the youth movement of the early decades of the twentieth century. There can be no doubt of what happened: the spirit of youth as youth protested against the spirit of capitalist society. That defines both the greatness and the limitations of the movement. It was great because the best forces of a whole generation revolted against the compulsions of a self-sufficient finitude; it was limited because the revolt was not inspired by a positive, prophetic power but by the vague longings of the youthful temper. The youth movement raised its protest against capitalist society at all the critical points; first of all—and in this the movement had its origin—it recovered the love of nature and deepened that love into a nature-mysticism with a decidedly religious coloring. Next it undertook to make a many-sided attack on the morals and immoralities of bourgeois convention, on Main Street naturalism as well as on Bohemian impressionism. In dress, speech, food and drink, dance, sociability, etc., the natural, the native and folklike, was emphasized. A romantic, religious relationship to the pre-capitalistic period, particularly to the Middle Ages, was gained. In the same fashion the youth movement recaptured in the sphere of human relations the mystical, religious ideal of community. Love of the community now takes the place of the social conflict. It is difficult to determine to what extent a sexual erotic element is present in this love; at all events this element had destructive effects only when it was consciously emphasized and given a central place in the social life, as happened in a few instances. In itself it is the necessary, unconscious power in all actual social life. Love of the community in the youth movement also had a mystical tinge and led youth back to an appreciation of the social theories of the past. A spontaneous development of leagues, of special relations to leaders, of chivalric romanticism, took place. The longings of the youth movement twined themselves around these things with great ardor and it raised questions and achieved insights in this connection which had been wholly lost to capitalist society.

It is intelligible why the youth movement, beginning with this background, rediscovered the mystical side of religion. The older mystical literature was cultivated in its circles and out of them came impulses toward a reform of Protestant worship in the direction of mysticism. It was not difficult for Catholicism to create within itself a youth movement which remained true to the church but which yet had contact with the other movements in the common love of mysticism and in the common opposition to the capitalist spirit. Ecclesiastical Protestantism was least affected of all by the youth movement because in its anti-mysticism and in its adult, masculine character it represents a type of mind which is antithetical to the spirit of the movement.

The crisis of the youth movement, in which we have lived for some time and which in some way indicates its decline, is due to the fact that the protest which it raised against the capitalist spirit was the protest of *youth*. Youth means revolt, longing, susceptibility; youth is destined to become adult, to achieve definite character and maturity. The turning point of the youth movement lies at the transition from youth to manhood; here the crisis begins. In this transition it became apparent that the movement had no structure of its own which it could oppose to the structure of capitalist society. The result, which could hardly be avoided, was that capitalist society took possession of the movement, both so far as individuals and as the whole were concerned. That the youth movement became political and was drawn into the existing parties of capitalist society is the external symptom of its actual decline. Yet it is impossible for youth simply to accept capitalist realism. When it represents this realism it has become a caricature of youth. But it is both possible and necessary for youth to adopt a *belief-ful realism*. It cannot be doubted that a longing for this realism is active in youth itself. Whither that longing will lead cannot be predicted. The result will depend on the form which will be discovered for this content. One can say, however, that with this change youth has approached the fundamental Protestant attitude and the strong influence which the neo-Protestant tendency in theology is exercising not only upon young theological students but on other young people is an indication of this fact. The main achievement of the youth movement for the religious situation of the present lies in the fact that the finest spirits in a whole generation revolted against the spirit of capitalist society and broke through the structure of a self-sufficient finitude. The vital energies which flow from this source into the social life are still the best and most important of all, and they continue to create an element of unrest and rebellion which has far from exhausted its influence and the religious meaning of which cannot easily be overestimated.

Among the many social problems which became alive again with the rediscovery of community-love the problems of the relations of the sexes, of healer and healed and of educator and educated are of particular importance for the contemporary religious situation. The last of these problems will be dealt with in connection with the whole subject of education.

Our present situation in sex-relations may be described in general by saying that the destruction of the sacramental character of marriage by Protestantism made marriage and all sex-relations a matter of the personal responsibility of individuals and subjected them at the same time to the divine natural law of exclusive monogamy. In capitalist society the divine law became a social convention, which permitted violations of exclusive monogamy almost without restrictions in the case of the husband, within limits in the case of the wife—so long as the validity of the convention itself was not challenged. Against the reign of this conventional hypocrisy an esthetic individualism, partly influenced by Nietzsche's powerful proclamation of the erotic, directed its attack. But this attack did not go far since it remained quite too individualistic and led to an unsocialized, erotic anarchy. In the proletariat also bourgeois convention was destroyed under the pressure of the economic atomization of society which did not stop even at the family and which, after abstracting the individuals of both sexes from their social nexus, arranged them as impersonal elements in the mechanical mass. It was inevitable then that in complete opposition to bourgeois morality unregulated sexual instinct should control sex relations. There was protest against bourgeois hypocrisy in this but the protest was based on the same foundations as the convention. No realization of eternal meanings present in the relation of the sexes was reached. The emancipation of woman from the remnants of early patriarchal custom, the fateful, historical development which threw her into the economic struggle, and her own achievement in attaining equality with men in culture and public life, constituted a third element in the movement. This also was still a consequence of capitalist society and its atomization of life, yet, like the other movements which dissolved bourgeois morality, it laid foundations for the rise of a new ideal of sex-relations. It was inevitable that attempts to realize a new ideal should be made first of all in complete freedom, without sacramental, religious and legal or conventional sanctions. The free, inner obligation of the mates to each other was made the ideal; to find it was an adventure, not commanded by law. Such a reconstruction of the sex-relation by the free individuals was undertaken by many persons with great sincerity and lofty idealism. Yet in practically every instance the impossibility of building up a sex morality in this way became apparent. Individuality can unite with individuality in living union only in the presence of a third, superior principle. And the only principle which is unconditionally super-ordinate is that which transcends time and change, the eternal. A community of life which does not rest on the foundation of the eternal is valid only for a time, even though this time coincide more or less accidentally with the total span of an individual life. But if it does so coincide that is an accident and one which does not frequently occur. This is one of the places where the misery of a self-sufficient finitude reveals itself in the tragic

fate of countless individuals and where it demands that breaking-through to the transcendent on which sex morality can be built anew.

A peculiar and, for the religious situation, important significance is attached in the present
to the art of healing. It must be recalled that
with the elimination of the priestly confessional
and the loss of its real values the physician
stepped upon the scene as a substitute. Yet he
was a substitute who could not supply what
should have been supplied, a healing process
proceeding out of man's central function, that
is, out of his religious relations. First of all the
separation of body and soul, then the mechanization of the body, then the conception of the
psychic as a product of the physical machine—
these logical consequences of a rationalistic, atomistic conception of nature which had been
deprived of life and of inwardness made the
healing art more and more a mechanical and
technical activity. The separate organs were
treated as though they were separate parts of a
machine which could be isolated; furthermore,
the body was treated and only the body. Even
the science of psychical healing came to be in
fact a science of physical healing or of the healing of separate organs. It is evident that according to this conception the relation of physician
and patient could only be an external, objective

and contractual relationship, not one of real community supported by love. Such a relationship corresponds to the fundamental lack of community-love in the spirit of capitalist society. In spite of all principles, it is true, authority upon the one hand and trust upon the other always played an important rôle and revealed their great significance, particularly in the treatment of psychic disorders. But it was only when the psycho-analytic method became effective after 1900 that more important consequences were realized. This method restores independence to the soul. The depths of the unconscious are explored independently of bodily and organic processes. Naturally such a procedure cannot be used unless the physician can enter sympathetically into the mind of the patient and this requires again that the patient have a personal *Eros*-attitude toward the physician (the attitude will oscillate between love and hate, and has nothing to do with eroticism, must in fact exclude this). Thus an important analogy to the old confessional relationship has been created. In the one as in the other decisive significance attaches to the soul's misery, which is almost always connected with guilt-complexes, to the relief brought by the recognition, verbal expression and the realization of hidden connections and, finally, to the determination to reconstruct the soul. Yet there is a profound difference between the two methods. In the confessional all this takes place in the presence of God. The mind is directed first of all to the eternal and only in the second place toward itself. The things confession is concerned with belong to the very heart of personality, to its freedom and responsibility. The danger of psycho-analysis is that it will deal with these same things from the point of view of natural occurrences and that it will constantly direct the attention of the patient to himself and his temporal existence. Thus the soul's center of gravity may be transferred from the center—from the point of personal responsibility in the presence of the Unconditioned—to the impersonal, unconscious, purely natural sphere. This is the source of the frequently destructive effects of psycho-analysis and the indication that in this instance also the self-sufficient finitude of the psychic has not been actually broken through. Only a priestly man can be a complete psychiatrist. For with him the relation to the patient and the inner activities of the patient have been lifted out of the realm of the subjectivity of the finite into the inclusive life of the eternal.

This is true not only of directly psychic disorders but, under certain conditions, also of physical disease. Insight into the dependence of all separate functions and separate organs on the total constitution and the further insight that this constitution is just as much a psychic as a physical fact make the healing of the body also a matter of community and love. The transmission of immediate healing powers was always practiced by certain individuals and groups in connection with the practice of orthodox medicine. It was practiced by men who had intuitive abilities in diagnosis and with the use of remedies which were admittedly only the symbols of the direct influence of person on person. The fight of orthodox medicine against medical romanticism is justified when it is directed against the latter's attempt to eliminate the technical treatment of the physical but it is not justified when it seeks to eliminate on its part the central mind-body, doctor-patient relationship and to exclude love and intuition. Yet a change in the conception of these relations is making itself evident at present in medical circles.

These things are significant for the religious situation of the present because the central, fundamental attitude of man is his religious attitude; hence the healing art must cease to be either merely parallel to or opposed to religion. When one remembers what imperative, continually effective significance the art of healing has for every man, almost without exception, it must seem almost incomprehensible that the special representatives of religion in the capitalist period paid so little attention to these things.

II. *Body and Soul.* It is pertinent to consider in this connection the efforts which are being made to promote the culture of the body. Four tendencies may be distinguished in this field: first, interest in gymnastic physical exercise; secondly, sport; thirdly, esthetic physical culture; and in the fourth place, the effort to achieve a unified development of the whole personality through physical development and discipline. The first type is regarded as a compensation for the one-sided intellectual emphasis in modern education. It rests, therefore, on the separation of body and mind and, while it is relatively justified, it does not lead to anything further. Physical culture as practiced in pure sport brings about the unbalanced development of certain physical functions and, for the champions, it becomes a professional interest which is rather far removed from the original idea of culture of the body. But the participation of enthusiastic followers in the rivalries of sport indicates a certain, frequently explicit, return to primitive esteem of physical power and visible heroism. That also is romanticism, the contradiction of the technical and mechanical view of the body, but it is not a contradiction which moves on a different level from that which is contradicted. Frequently enough it moves upon a lower level and shows to how great an extent the upper and the lower masses of capitalist society have been robbed of a genuine, substantial spirituality and corporeality. The esthetic form of physical culture is primarily devoted to the service of the dance and has been dealt with. The fourth tendency has real significance for the future; it seeks to overcome, in principle, the antithesis of the physical and the spiritual and to develop the culture of the body into an education of the total personality. It is highly significant that in culturally important groups there is a wide-spread interest in rhythmic gymnastics as an aid to a new rhythmic sense of life, with metaphysical implications; carried on therefore not just as a matter of physical technique but as involving the whole person. Ideas about the rhythm of life such as Fritz Klatt has expressed in his book about the "creative pause" belong to this field. Naturally there is no lack of romanticism in these things and there is imminent danger that a movement which begins with the physical and neglects the whole psychic attitude will fall back into a technique of the physical or into mere estheticism. For the rest it is worth noting that the ideal which is arising in this movement is, so far as one can judge, not the classical ideal. What is sought is not so much the perfection of the body but rather a somehow mystical, concentrated and emanative force which shapes the mind and body; but the fundamental asceticism associated with older forms of this mysticism is lacking.

III. *Educational and Moral Ideals.* The problem of the culture of the body in the broad sense belongs to the problem of education which is the last of the social problems we intend to examine for the sake of defining their religious significance. The pedagogy of capitalist society was conditioned by two presuppositions: on the one hand, the loss of a content determined by the reference of life to the eternal and the consequent attention to finite forms; on the other hand, the loss of community-love and the consequent separation of the subject and the object of educational activity. The result was a series of phenomena which are characteristic of the spirit of capitalist society as the spirit of self-sufficient finitude. Formally the character of capitalist education was revealed by the fact that nature and tradition were regarded not from the point of view of their meaning, as referring to the eternal, but from the point of view of their finite, phenomenal form. Consequently the materials of education were to be received intellectually, through knowledge of the finite and phenomenal form. Scientific and formal esthetic interests stood and still stand in the forefront in all educational enterprise. The excellent thing about this type of education is the training in objectivity, judicial moderation and truthfulness which is connected with it. Its limitation lies in the fact that it deprives things of their vital meaning for life and for the present. History is regarded unmythologically and as quite foreign to the present; nature is robbed of its intrinsic vitality and looked upon as something which is to be technically controlled. Professional education is distinguished from general education only by the fact that it is directed toward one practical end. It is the really logical form of education in capitalist society and for that reason the most highly developed and successful form. General education, on the other hand, is lifted above intellectualism to really spiritual excellence only with the aid of esthetic appreciation in the case of very few individuals. But this attitude also has an ultimately irresponsible character. The masses are excluded from such education. Those who press toward it are little more than the left-over remnants of bourgeois education. For the rest, the proletariat feels that the real meaning of capitalist education lies partly in the preparation for admission to the upper class of society, partly in the capitalization of knowledge for technical purposes and the extension of power. And the proletariat itself has a sufficient portion of the capitalist temper to desire a share in this capital of knowledge.

All movements against the spirit of capitalist society in education are united in their opposition to the intellectualism of purely formal training. The difficulties which these movements encounter are due to the fact that every type of education is ultimately dependent upon the spiritual meaning which determines what its goals and methods are to be. There is, to be sure, in pedagogy and in the relationship of teacher and taught, a rational, in theory universally valid, element. It is the basis of scientific pedagogy which must therefore be regarded as a typical product of the capitalist spirit. This situation naturally makes it extraordinarily difficult to overcome that spirit in education since that means also to overcome pedagogy as a rational science. It is true that most of the movements of revolt in education are directed against formal pedagogy but they do not recognize that they are; they operate along the lines of this pedagogy and thus keep it alive. Now every educational method which does not rest upon a common relationship of both teacher and taught to something ultimate, to the eternal, is inadequate. For in the sphere of the finite every goal that is set up, every method which is employed, is doubtful, limited, ultimately irresponsible. Only the Unconditioned can create unconditioned responsibility and therewith a relationship of teacher and taught which rests upon mutual responsibility and the possibility of unqualified loyalty. Given this common basis, the technique of communicating forms, which is the real problem of scientific pedagogy, becomes a question of the second order.

This insight is particularly important for social education, for it offers the solution of the problem of mass education which is insoluble for formal pedagogy. The folk-high-school movement of the post-war years struggled with this problem and after great, external successes in the beginning suffered severe reversals. The problem, in the form in which this movement formulated it, was insoluble. It is true that the plan of carrying the bourgeois culture to the masses or to a selected group was opposed at once by the leaders of the movement. But the question then arose as to what was to be substituted for this culture. And now it appeared that the only thing possible was to make a philosophy of the world and life the basis of education and to develop this philosophy in the coöperative thinking of teachers and pupils. The confessional religious groups could easily answer the question as to which philosophy was to be made fundamental, but the remaining groups had no other alternative than to seek and, if luck were with them, to find their way through all the conflicting philosophies. On the whole they did not and, in the nature of the case, could not succeed. Therefore the denominational high-schools flourished while the others remained far behind their ambitiously projected goals. The spirit of capitalist society had only been strengthened. But the attempt to make the whole anti-capitalistic movement productive for the development of an educational ideal and method will not be abandoned. The attempt may be made more from the side of aristocratic, individual education or more from the side of mass education. Religious socialism is making an emphatic effort on the social side in connection with the religious forces which had been buried in the labor movement. To what extent it will be possible to set these forces free again and to discover a new, unconditionedly imperative basis on which they can build their educational ideal and method remains a question which the future only can answer.

Not only social and political efforts are to be considered in this connection but also the great and general reform movements such as are being promoted by the League of School Reformers, and similar movements. Among these also a passionate attack is being made upon capitalist education. The authoritative communication of the subject matter is opposed; originality and creative activity on the part of the pupil are encouraged. Vital participation of the pupil in perceptual reality is to take the place of the intellectual communication of the rational and abstract form of things. Fellowship between the pupils and between them and the teacher is proclaimed as the ideal form of the educational relationship. This is all of great importance for the religious situation of the present and particularly of the future. Love of community and love of things are beginning to prevail in contrast to the capitalist social relations and attitudes toward things. Yet permanent failures also occur. The fundamental presupposition for the realization of all these demands is present only in desire, not in fact. What is missing is a tangible, wholly obligatory, basic and holy meaning of the educational ideal and method. As long as this is missing and to the extent to which it is missing anti-capitalist pedagogy will be in a difficult position and will remain more a signpost toward the future than a creative force in the present. In this case also realism and faith are necessary, not romanticism and fanaticism.

Back of the question about the educational ideal and relationship and back of all problems in the practical sphere, lies ultimately the question about ethics, i.e., the question about activity directed toward the Unconditioned. The ethical attitude corresponds in the practical sphere to the metaphysical attitude in the theoretic and ethics like metaphysics has been destroyed under the reign of the capitalist spirit. The ethical ideal which capitalist society took over from the Renaissance and Humanism was the ideal of humanity. Two elements are present in this principle: it means, on the one hand, all possible human values and, on the other hand, the incorporation of these values in an organized, social form. Even the relationship to the eternal belongs to the human values and receives its place as part of the spiritual unity. The idea of humanity is not irreligious but it contains the antithesis to the directly religious consciousness, for the latter breaks up the unity of the spiritual structure for the sake of man's relation to the eternal and arouses the conflict within the spirit which arises necessarily from the relationship of temporal and eternal, of God and world. In contrast to this division which is essential to the religious consciousness the ideal of humanity must be described as the ideal of a self-sufficient finitude.

The ideal of humanity develops in two directions, in relation to individuals on the one hand, to society on the other. In the case of the individual the ideal is one of a spiritually perfected, autonomous personality; in the case of society it is the ideal of the free association of the greatest possible number of the most highly developed individuals. To both ideals the same criticism applies which must be made of the ideal of humanity in general—in them the relation to the eternal is one element among others, or even above others, but it does not mean that all the functions of the individual personality or of the community are called into question by something eternal. The ideal of humanity emancipates personality and society from the demons of old, sacramental custom. Human kind is lifting itself up, out of subhuman and inhuman religion among other things. What is lost, however, is the super-human, the religious questioning of human sufficiency, the judgment upon even the perfected human spirit. The ethics of humanity like the metaphysics of humanity reduces the relation to the eternal to a human and finite function. And that means the destruction of the function.

The criticism offered by Nietzsche was more penetrating; it set the ideal of an aristocratic and meaningful personality in contrast to the bourgeois personality. Race-theories, conceptions of national excellence and romantic ideas of nobility and leadership were frequently combined with it as in the case of Spengler, for it is this ethics which forms the background of his philosophy of history. But while there was in Nietzsche's symbol of the super-man a reference to the transcendently Unconditioned these modern movements remain almost completely thisworldly. Therefore this ethics is easily and frequently combined with the ethics of the will-to-power and of the successful, economic, capitalist conqueror. Rarely is the circle of the finite transcended. Naturalism, often of a brutal sort, is dominant and what goes beyond this is usually entirely romantic.

The idea of community which arises out of religious and romantic thought must be taken more seriously. It has rejected the capitalist and old socialist ideal of happiness and has set forth an ideal of community and personality which has transcendent references and which every one, quite apart from his cultural background and education, is able to realize. But these ideals lack a typical realization which would have the force of a symbol; the lack is inevitable for such realizations can come only out of religion. An ethics can come to fulfillment only as a religious ethics. Therefore the ethics of the anti-capitalistic movement remains provisional, insecure and expectant in all cases and always falls prey again to capitalist morality. Only if the ideal of humanity instead of being denied were given a measure of self-transcendence in vision and in realization would the ethics of self-sufficient finitude be broken through.

Our consideration of the practical sphere has revealed that the religious situation in it is even more completely dominated by the spirit of capitalist society than is the case in the theoretic sphere. This lies in the nature of the case. When the spirit is moved in those depths which lie beneath the antithesis of theory and practice it achieves a definite form of consciousness first of all in seeing and foreseeing contemplation. The shaping of concrete reality follows and follows necessarily; for it is the same spirit which is effective in pre-vision and in transformation. Only the certainty that this is so can offer defiance to the actual and growing power of the spirit of self-sufficient finitude. Only it can offer opposition to a weak and arbitrary realism which worships that which is because it is, and which does not know that reality cannot hold its ground when the idea, the depth of the spirit, has been revolutionized. (Hegel.) That it has been revolutionized can be seen, despite all the powerful resistance offered by the practical sphere, in that sphere itself.

Part Three

THE CONTEMPORARY RELIGIOUS
SITUATION IN RELIGION

ONE

MYSTICISM OUTSIDE THE CHURCHES

I. *Esthetic Mysticism.* If our two presuppositions are correct, that the relation of time and eternity is effective in all spheres of spiritual life and that under the rule of the capitalist spirit leadership devolved entirely upon the cultural sphere, then the most important part of our task has been accomplished; the fundamental answer to questions about the religious situation of our time has been given. It is highly characteristic of our period that it is possible to give this answer without touching upon the specifically religious sphere. The most important religious movements are developing outside of religion.

Yet it is impossible that these movements should not react upon the religious sphere in the narrower sense of the term. Just because religion has become so largely dependent on the cultural process, the latter should be visibly reflected in the former. This is actually the case and, furthermore, a consideration of the religious situation in the religious sphere has the additional advantage of revealing more directly and clearly the processes with which we have been dealing. For it is the distinctive characteristic of religion that it explicitly intends and expresses in concrete symbols the reference of time to eternity. Religion seeks to be direction of the conditioned toward the Unconditioned. It stands in essential antithesis, therefore, to a culture whose fundamental principle is the self-sufficiency of the finite. It stands in essential antithesis to the spirit of capitalist society. All the more difficult does its position become in a period which is dominated by this spirit. Under the circumstances only two possibilities are open to religion. It may seek to maintain itself in all its ancient forms with their reference to the eternal, and with them stand in opposition to the self-sufficient forms of culture. It may form a more or less limited sphere of fundamental opposition. This is what orthodox or clerical ecclesiasticism did, but at the same time it allowed itself to be forced to the very borders of the region in which the actual historical process went on and it became internally sterile. The other possibility is that religion become hospitable to the forms of the capitalist culture, take up within itself the opposition to itself, enter into the most difficult conflicts and be driven ultimately to complete surrender. That was the fate of liberal Protestantism, liberal Judaism and Catholic Modernism. These antitheses were the ruling factors in the religious situation within the churches. The alternatives seemed inescapable and came to be fateful for the religious life. It was possible to overcome the situation only if two approaches were made at the same time, the approach from culture and the approach from the church. In culture the system of self-sufficient finite forms needed to be broken and the way to the Unconditioned sought out. In religion the identification of the Unconditioned with definite forms of the past needed to be abandoned while its unconditioned character in the face of time and all existent things was not given up. Both approaches have been made and have found each other to an increasing degree. They run together more and more despite the tension that exists between them.

The approach from culture to religion has been examined. The way from religion to culture now demands attention. But as soon as we turn to it we note that it has two aspects. On the one hand there are intra-churchly movements, on the other hand a series of extra-ecclesiastical religious movements which doubtless influence the complexion of the present to a greater degree than do the former. We must begin therefore with the latter, particularly since they may be regarded to a certain extent as mediating movements between culture and religion.

When we seek to classify the numerous religious movements of our day the following point of view suggests itself: the relation of the finite to the infinite, of the temporal to the eternal, may be conceived in two ways. Either the eternal may be regarded as the present, as that which supports and fills the present and its temporal forms with meaning; or it may be conceived as that which stands beyond all time and every temporal form, which lays its demands upon them and judges them. Both ideas are contained in the essence of the eternal and of its relation to time. Both require expression and the whole history of religion is the history of a struggle to reconcile the two tendencies. The first tendency is realized in mysticism—in pure mysticism as well as in the mysticism of worship and the sacraments. The other tendency is present in the eschatological movements in which the hope of an other-worldly perfection is combined with the thought of the demand and judgment made by the eternal. We shall consider, therefore, first the mystical and then the eschatological religious movements outside of the churches.

It is quite understandable that the first reaction against the spirit of capitalist society should come from the side of mysticism. For capitalist society is the final result of a process which was thoroughly anti-mystical. It grew out of the numerous late medieval reactions against Catholic sacramentalism. Its power lay in the will to subject the world to the divine demand and to place individual personality in its essence, immediately before the presence of God. But this was at the same time the reason for its loss of a present God and it led to the slow impoverishment of religion and to devotion to the finite forms. Through the loss of the priestly spirit, of the mystical, worshipful atmosphere which nurtured and maintained all life and in which the whole personality, not only its central essence, lived and moved, the rise of a secular, capitalist society became possible. Consequently reactions against that society made the mystic spirit of the past their point of departure.

One forerunner among others of this reaction was Johannes Mueller. With his proclamation of the immediacy of life he opposed the materialization and rationalization of reality in bourgeois philosophy as well as in ecclesiastical theology. He sought to free the fountains of the inner life by removing the débris of things and he exercised a truly priestly effect on not a few members of the younger generation. He freed them of the burden of merely conceptual antitheses and gave religious life its own independent foundations. His conception of life, to be sure, remained finite and subjective so that it was impossible for this attack upon capitalist society really to break through the lines of the finite.

The rediscovery of the ancient mystics was of greater importance. Meister Eckhart, the women mystics of the Middle Ages, the stories of the saints, the Franciscan legend, the Protestant mysticism of Angelus Silesius—all this material was offered in readable form and was welcomed by all cultured groups. Russian influences, such as Soloviev's mystical philosophy and Dostoievski's descriptions of Russian monasticism in *The Brothers Karamazov* became effective. The movement went beyond the boundaries of Western culture. Just as mysticism in principle seeks to rise above all form to the nameless One, so the mystical movement sought to transcend the forms of Christian Europe and to feel its kinship with India and

China. The high esteem in which the Brahmanic religion of the Upanishads and the doctrines of Maya and Nirvana were held had come down from Schopenhauer and the French decadence. To be sure, the modern pessimistic strain which was discovered as a result of this approach in Indian religion has been shown to be a Western importation. In general the positive meaning of Nirvana has been recognized and Indian mysticism in consequence has approached more closely to Western mysticism. But a very great impression was made by the personality of Buddha and by early Buddhism, so that Buddhist communities even were organized in Europe. More recently Lao-tse has taken a place alongside of Buddha; the difficulty of translating his ambiguous utterances makes it possible to understand him in a very modern, though certainly historically inadequate, sense.

As a result of all these influences an atmosphere was created in which immediate certainty attached to a mystical conception of God. The materialistic and atheistic solutions of the problem of God appeared more and more to be wholly erroneous and impossible. But a real pantheism also, as it was represented by the monistic movement, which in spirit belongs wholly to the nineteenth century, received no attention in the more highly educated circles. The mystical view of the world was victorious along the whole line. The only exception was formed by the proletariat in which free religious communities, free-thinkers and leagues of friends of nature continued the naturalistic tradition of bourgeois society as it existed in the eighties and nineties of the past century, though under the influence of Boelsche and others a decidedly romantic and esthetic coloring has been given the tradition. Among the intellectual leaders, however, these things have long ago been consigned to the vanished past. It is clear why it was mysticism which helped the twentieth century to recover the certainty of God. The difficulty of the religious situation lay in the fact that the concepts in which the God-idea had been expressed, religiously or philosophically, had been wholly destroyed or rendered powerless. A weak ecclesiastical apologetic, constantly in retreat, had served to rob the old concepts still further of the esteem in which they had previously been held. A decisive change in this field was not to be thought of. Such a change could only take place if, beyond all conceptual forms, the immediate reality of the religious factor were discovered and envisioned in vital fashion. In this process mysticism was the logical guide. For it is itself the product of the disintegration of old cult-forms and an attempt to find, beyond all forms, union with the divine ground.

But highly as the positive achievement of modern mysticism for the rediscovery of an immediate consciousness of God must be valued, a low estimate must be made of its ability to create religious forms. Therein its fundamental difference from ancient mysticism comes to light. The latter came out of the development of a positive, concrete religion and remained in close contact with that faith. The old mystic went beyond cult and sacrament but he did not criticize them. The modern mystic, on the other hand, uses mysticism in order to set positive religion completely aside. The esthetic character of the modern type which distinguishes it in its inner essence from the ancient form is connected with this fact. It is not an accident that it is being transmitted primarily in fine literature, partly in new productions, partly in esthetic presentations of ancient literature. It lacks that vital seriousness which always made the ancient mystic an ascetic at the same time. Ultimately it remains confined within the esthetic form and so reveals the fact that the spirit of self-sufficient finitude is stronger in it than is the desire to break through to the eternal. The modern mystic does not seek the ascetic isolation of the genuine mystic, who always remains loyal to the cult-group out of which he has come, but continues in bourgeois individualism and often uses mysticism only for the purpose of refining and increasing that individualism. Wherever, as in the youth movement, groups with a mystical coloring were formed the bond of union was not religion but the national ideal or a formless love of fellowship.

II. *Occult Mysticism.* Actual community organization was achieved by mysticism in only one sphere and that by a type which must be regarded as of inferior rank, the occult type. Occultism is the epitome of all those ideas and actions which refer to a reality which is hidden to the natural consciousness. The question whether such a reality exists cannot be raised here; at all events it is impossible to disprove its existence. But what is important for our evaluation of the religious situation is the question what the relationship of such an occult world-between-the-worlds would be to the religious sphere. On this point it may be said that what religion means—that is the divine—is the absolutely hidden, that which transcends all experience, including occult experience. In the presence of the eternal even the occult is temporal, this-worldly, finite. In and of itself the occult sphere has no religious meaning. Like the world of experience it is subject to the judgment of the eternal and it is like the former also in that it may serve to veil the eternal.

Spiritualism—the attempt to enter into actual relations with the souls of the dead—is quite apparently outside the sphere of religion. Even the proof of immortality, which spiritualism—if its explanation of spiritualist phenomena should be true—would seem to offer, has only an indirectly religious significance. It puts primitive materialism to shame, to be sure, but the real question, the question as to the eternity of the soul, its transcendence even of occult temporality, is not proved thereby; that remains indemonstrable even for occultism.

Astrology, in case it should be based in some way on some truth, is an intuition of the interconnection of the world, working with a peculiar method directly contradictory to the method of science; but it is as such not a religious view of the world.

The field of magic influences exercised by person on person, or by person on things, stands for a certain psycho-technical ability to apprehend and to influence. But this also lies outside the realm of actual religion, even though the ability be abused in demonic fashion. The exaltation of consciousness into higher states, the revelation of higher relations of being, such as

Theosophy and Anthroposophy teach and practice, may lead indeed to a very comprehensive and self-consistent view of the world. And this view may approach very closely to Neo-Platonic mysticism; one may speak of a vision of ideas in God. But when that has been admitted its distinction from genuine mysticism is all the more evident. Mysticism, including the Neo-Platonic sort, in its ultimate and first postulate breaks through the world of mind and idea to the abyss which lies beyond all forms. It knows of the leap which must be made out of time, even supra-mundane time, into eternity. Theosophy and Anthroposophy have a religious character only when they also rise above the intermediate world. Otherwise they achieve a view of the world which may be highly symbolic of the divine and which to that extent stands in antithesis to the spirit of capitalist society, but they do not attain to a really religious attitude.

Rudolf Steiner has developed the philosophical character of occult intuition in comprehensive fashion. There is hardly a sphere of reality which he has not considered and interpreted anew from the point of view of occult experience. In peculiar fashion he combines occult tradition with Western rationalism in this attempt. Furthermore, he has organized the Anthroposophists into a community, the members of which have all the external marks of fanatic religious sectarians. Still one cannot speak even in this case of a truly religious movement. It is true that Steiner has understood the tendency in the modern spirit which contradicts the spirit of the nineteenth century at every point, but the source of his creative activity is not religion but occult intuition. It remains this-worldly. Because it claims, nevertheless, to have religious quality, it is characterized by that peculiar fanaticism which always arises when something limited and finite lays claim to divinity.

Yet even within Anthroposophy there must have been a feeling that the religious problem was not really solved by it. The so-called "Christian Fellowship" (*Christengemeinschaft*) in which the specifically religious element was to be explicitly realized split off from it. In this movement Steiner's principles are vitalized through the use of ritual forms and by being related to the seven Catholic sacraments. A priesthood, which justifies its right to existence by pleading the new revelation of the spiritual world in Steiner, gathers small congregations whose central rite is the consecration of man. Even the name of this sacrament, but above all its forms, indicate that the spirit which is effective in it is not the Christian spirit. Christ is regarded as a being coming out of the intermediate world. The paradox of the cross, that God is present in an actual human body and that it is just in suffering that his majesty is revealed—this fundamental Christian conception is missing. Christ does not reach up to God nor down to man but remains between the two. Occult intuition and rationalistic speculation about the Christ-mind take the place of faith in the divine paradox. In this instance also the philosophic sphere is not really transcended. Still it must be recognized that the "Christian Fellowship" tends to meet the mystical, priestly longings of the time. For this reason it achieved some not inconsiderable successes in the beginning, even among the evangelical clergy, but it appears to have passed its zenith.

What has been said about Anthroposophy applies, with some limitations, to all movements in which occult and religious elements are amalgamated. Groups such as the Christian Scientists, the Healers (*Gesundbeter*), Mazdanan, etc., which are founded on the mysticism of the will, on breathing technique and similar bases, probably reach the occult but not the religious world in principle. In this mysticism of the second order intensification of human consciousness is always confused with the religious attitude. Self-sufficient finitude has been split; it is divided into a lower and a higher sphere, but it is not transcended, for even the higher world remains *world*, while in genuine mysticism the world in all its degrees vanishes in the presence of the invisible Beyond, of the Eternal itself. Occultism as such cannot overcome the spirit of self-sufficient finitude. It can loosen the hold of that finitude at many places; it can point to the world of true essences, but it cannot go beyond that. Significant as it is for the religious situation of the present, so limited is its fundamental religious meaning.

TWO

ESCHATOLOGICAL MOVEMENTS

Eschatological movements stand alongside the mystic movements of the first and second rank. They are also almost exclusively non-ecclesiastical but in their structure and in numerous elements taken over from tradition they show a much closer relationship to the churches than do mystic individualism or occultism. Nevertheless the situation in this case also was such that the most effective expression of the eschatological expectation was not religious prophecy but philosophy of history, as presented particularly in Spengler's calculations of European decline and in the Communist hope of a coming ideal community. Both of these are to be considered only insofar as they were preparatory for the directly religious eschatological mood. Capitalist society had substituted the idea of

173

progress for the idea of the end of the world. For the spirit of self-sufficient finitude there is no such thing as an end in the definite sense of the term, since the end means the real catastrophe of all finitude which is sufficient to itself. For this reason the strongest, the religiously most decisive challenges to time, have come out of the great prophecies of the end. For the end is the expression of the essential relationship between time and eternity.

Nietzsche's prediction of the rise of a European nihilism was transformed by Spengler into a prophecy of the decline of Western civilization. The procedure was logical. For whenever the biological point of view is applied to the rise and decay of cultures the decay of a high civilization must be taken into calculation as an inevitable fate. Nietzsche did not take it into calculation; he did not calculate at all; he believed. He believed in the miracle of a new, savior race, the creative aristocracy. He did not indicate, to be sure, how a wholly exhausted life-force could produce such a miracle. Spengler calculated and did not believe, hence he had to calculate the end. But in the background of his calculations there was also a faith—faith, namely, in the biological character of spirit or, what amounts to the same thing, disbelief in the spirit as a creative force. In consequence Spengler could be effective only there where self-sufficient finitude had seen through itself, negatively and resignedly, at best stoically. Yet for many men this negation offered the basis for a new position. Many of the religious movements which make the conception of a turn in time their chief symbol, have been indirectly influenced by Spengler's European pessimism—though they have converted it into an optimistic expectation of the end.

The eschatological movements of the socialist and revolutionary sort are directly positive and optimistic. Insofar as they have not been weakened by fatigue or the tactics of reform, that is by the spirit of capitalist society, they are supported by the spirit of Utopianism. But Utopianism is direction to the eternal conceived as the goal of this-worldly activity. In all Utopianism there is an element of faith, a transcending of the finite. But insofar as it is Utopianism it also contains unbelief and bondage to the finite. As a result of this unbelief, this inability to break through to the Unconditioned beyond time, the religious enthusiasm of Utopianism is lost and—regarded in retrospect as the product of disappointment—is replaced by progress or reaction.

The most important source of religious socialism lies in the effort to overcome the unbelieving element in Utopian socialism, the bondage to the finite and temporal, without abolishing the eschatological enthusiasm. This double intention has been expressed in the idea of "Kairos." Kairos is fulfilled time, the moment of time which is invaded by eternity. But Kairos is not perfect completion in time. To act and wait in the sense of Kairos means to wait upon the invasion of the eternal and to act accordingly, not to wait and act as though the eternal were a fixed quantity which could be introduced into time, as a social structure which represents the end and goal of history, for instance. The eternal is that which invades; it is not something tangible and objective. There are societies which are turned away from the eternal, which rest content in time and finiteness, and there are other societies which are turned toward the eternal and which express in their forms the judgment which they have experienced as proceeding from it. But there are no societies which possess the eternal. According to religious socialism, therefore, the only goal which our eschatological hope can look forward to is this, that the judgment proceeding from the eternal may result in an organization of life and society in which the orientation toward the eternal is recognizable. The concept of Kairos expresses a belief-ful realism in contrast to unbelieving realism and to belief-ful or Utopian idealism. One of the most important questions for the religious situation of the future is the question whether socialism as a whole will attain to the attitude of a belief-ful realism.

We enter the directly religious sphere when we turn to the consideration of the eschatological religious sects which seek and find their adherents particularly among Protestants. The individual sect and its peculiarities are of no significance for the total situation, but the effect of all of them together—Adventists, New Apostolic Churches, Bible Students, Weissenbergers and many others—is an important criterion of our situation. In general two elements characterize the eschatological sect: the eschatological hope and an especially intensive community life. The hope of the consummation occupies the foreground. It is the form in which the direction toward the eternal is symbolically represented. It supplies the movement with that enthusiasm and impulsive force which it has for many who have come to grief in their struggle with finitude. This form of eschatological gospel is particularly effective in the case of men who neither find saving powers in the finite nor expect a coming salvation in its sphere, but who lack the religious ability to recognize the actual transcendence of the eternal and who therefore hope for a temporal, visually conceived, final catastrophe. Today as in all other periods this attitude finds receptive minds especially in lower middle class groups. But many individuals in the laboring class also are driven into such movements by the disappointment of their Utopian hopes. That these ideas, however, will be able to exercise any decisive influence on wider circles either in the laboring class or in the more highly educated groups must be considered out of the question. For that result the position is too dubious in its vacillation between time and eternity; it offers too little to either. Eschatological hopes are religiously important only when they appear in union with religiously creative forces as in the New Testament period, for instance. In the case of contemporary movements it is impossible to speak of such a union.

The other element which characterizes every sect is the concrete, limited community life which it can realize in a way that is impossible for a national church or a cultural community. The active participation of every one in worship and in the life of the community, mutual aid within and beyond the group, voluntary membership, the personal responsibility of every individual, the simplicity and symbolic effectiveness of the message, the consciousness of belonging to the circle of the elect—all these things have a powerful appeal for numerous men with religious needs who have been left untouched or have been repelled by the church. They are ineffective, however, in circles where a higher cultural development is demanded than prevails in the sectarian circles or where secular communities satisfy similar needs. The sectarian movement is limited above all by the fact that its precondition is a definite, relatively rare, attitude of mind. Consequently it is not to be expected that the eschatological communities will win any decisive significance for the total religious situation. They also act disintegratingly and stand in opposition, therefore, to capitalist society. In their individualism, however, they are definitely akin to that spirit and, for that matter, capitalist society contains a not inconsiderable spiritual heritage derived from the Protestant sect.

Religious socialism was in danger for a time of turning into a pietistic, eschatological sect. In that case it would have lost its meaning as a comprehensive and far-reaching movement. Above all else it would have lost all possibility of influencing the mass-movement of socialism. Every sect contains the demonism of Pharisaism. When contrasted to the sect the spirit of capitalist society does not appear to be wholly wrong. The only kind of eschatological movement which can be superior to that spirit must be a movement which does not have regard to itself but which looks to the eternal toward which it is directed, which is, therefore, truly free and free also for the masses.

THREE

THE RELIGIOUS SITUATION
IN THE CHURCHES

I. *Catholicism.* The fundamental difficulty in the situation of the churches today is due to the inner antagonism between religion and capitalist society. We have considered the beginnings of the movement to overcome this antagonism as it proceeded from the side of culture. An approach is also being made, as we have seen, in the religious movements outside the churches. Our final task is the consideration of the way in which the churches themselves are seeking to adjust themselves to the fundamental problem in their situation. Theoretically there are three possibilities: the denial of the capitalist spirit, surrender to it, and the attempt to overcome it on the basis of its own presuppositions. All three forms are present in both the Catholic and Protestant churches, but the Catholic church is by nature inclined to reject the capitalist spirit while Protestantism tends rather to seek union with it.

Since the Counter-Reformation Catholicism has been fighting a defensive war directed equally against Protestantism on the one hand and autonomous civilization on the other. In contrast to both of these the medieval form of religious, spiritual and social life, as theoretically formulated by Thomas Aquinas, is regarded as the ideal. But the religious situation in both the early and middle periods of medievalism was the direct antithesis in every point to the religious situation prevailing in the reign of capitalist society. The former in all its forms and symbols was directed toward the eternal. In principle it acknowledged no self-sufficient finite entity either in science or in economics, either in law or in political life. It might seem therefore that the defeat of the capitalist spirit would lead men back to a new medievalism, back necessarily into the Catholic church. The extraordinarily strong sense of victorious power which prevails in contemporary Catholicism rests upon this conviction. It believes that it can see the approach of its hour of triumph. There is a general turning away from the capitalist spirit. Protestantism is in a very difficult situation. The period of separation from the priestly mother church is over. All Catholic literature is full of these ideas and they are made practically effective in propaganda and in ecclesiastical missionary activity.

In this connection of the universalist character of Catholicism, its idea of a religious culture, is important. It allows the church to express its opinions in the political sphere through party-organizations such as the Center party in Germany and corresponding parties in other countries and in the sphere of theory, in science and art, through journals such as *Hochland* and others. In both respects Protestantism is in an entirely different position and even its attempts to found Protestant literary journals, such as *Die Zeitwende*, will be unable to change the situation despite the interest which these attempts deserve. The simple reason for this fact is that Protestantism does not possess an independent culture apart from capitalist society.

The various fundamental tendencies in the Catholic attitude follow from the application of the medieval ideal to the present situation. The idea of humanity is accepted on the basis of the idea of a unified Christendom, not in a democratic, idealistic sense but from the point of view of a religious, hierarchical unity to which the individual nations are to subordinate themselves. Nationalism in either the liberal or conservative form is rejected. In internal political relations the ruling idea is that of organic structure, again not in the conservative and aristocratic sense but as a Christian solidarity—a term which is being used at present not without considerable distortion of its original meaning. The unifying principle in the social structure is the church with its hierarchical order superior to all mundane powers. By this means the class-conflict is to be overcome. It is scarcely possible to oppose capitalism directly in the economic life. But the whole temper of the Catholic world is unfavorable to the capitalist principle. It does not thrive there as well as it does on Protestant, Jewish or Humanist soil. With reference to the separate social problems the church emphasizes medieval ethics as strongly as possible and frequently in opposition to the customary social views of the day. The Catholic youth movement has developed with particular vitality; in general it is analogous to the rest of the youth movement but emphasizes the mystic side more strongly. At this point, but not only here, a romantic Catholicism is growing up; it has a peculiar charm even for many non-Catholics and enters into the anti-capitalist movement in many instances.

Catholicism is developing less impressively in

the theoretical than in the practical spheres. Its vitality and adaptability are less considerable in this field, for here it is bound, in science and philosophy by dogma and the authority of the church, in art by the ritual and its tradition. Nevertheless an indirect influence is evident in this case also. The rediscovery of the art of the early Middle Ages, the growing interest of modern philosophy in scholasticism, the importance of medieval, intuitive conceptual realism for the contemporary phenomenological school—all these indicate that the Catholic spirit is exerting an influence such as would have been impossible even a few years ago.

After all that has been said it might seem as though the Catholic church were the leading power in the battle against the spirit of capitalist society. It possesses the great uninterrupted tradition which derives from the spiritual situation of the pre-capitalist period. At the same time it possesses a positive content which makes it superior to all other movements of antagonism to the spirit of self-sufficient finitude. This judgment, however, which is also the judgment Catholicism is making about its future, is inadmissible from the point of view of our interpretation of the day. We have seen that even the spirit of capitalist society contains elements which were originally derived from prophetic vision and which were only gradually secularized. Catholicism has ignored these elements. At decisive points it has remained aloof from the destructive invasions of the eternal. For the church the only sphere in which there can be an invasion of the eternal is its doctrine and its ritual. The eternal is bound to a certain, temporal entity, to the church and its tradition. That means that the church itself has fallen prey in a certain fashion to the spirit of self-sufficient finitude. It has lost the vitality, the directness and receptiveness which it had preserved until late in the medieval period. As a result of its defensive attitude against Protestantism and Humanism it has allowed itself to become an objective, fixed, finite entity. In Jesuitism particularly the rationalism of the church's finite and, at the same time, endless will-to-power achieved a complete expression, similar in many respects to growing capitalism. The church became a piece of self-sufficient finitude and therewith really resigned rulership to the spirit of capitalist society. It could have conquered the latter only if it had been ready to give up its claims to its own absoluteness and inviolability.

There are no indications of any sort that it is ready to surrender these claims. Catholic theology is being confined by the church within ever narrower limits; the scientific interpretation of Scripture is made impossible, systematic theology must accept Saint Thomas as its unalterable norm. The central, papal power is being constantly strengthened; the pope is regarded not only as the chief bishop but as the universal bishop—a change which has taken place only recently and which excludes the possibility of episcopal counter-actions against the rule of the curia. Movements in favor of a reform of the ritual are concerned only with its psychological and esthetic aspects. The substantial content remains unchanged and labor on its form results only in reappropriations of ancient material, not in new creation. Wherever there are movements which might develop into real revolts against Counter-Reformation Catholicism they are tolerated only so long as they are of value for purposes of propaganda. As soon as they become dangerous to the centralization and the absoluteness of the church they are destroyed. When and how this fate will come upon the romantic Catholicism of our time cannot be predicted. But it is certain that unless romantic Catholicism calls a halt to its development in time this fate will visit it also. Whether it will then be able to summon up the power for a creative, intra-catholic movement is very doubtful. At all events ecclesiastically limited Catholicism, petrified and mechanized in its forms, is not the superior antagonist of the spirit of capitalist society for which it is often mistaken. But it is only this kind of Catholicism that can be considered seriously in our review of the present situation.

The situation in Greek Catholicism is quite different. It did not pass through Reformation, Humanism and Counter-Reformation. It belongs to a time which preceded the period of petrifaction and rationalization. It stands upon the level of a primitive mysticism and sacramentalism which men of the capitalist period cannot possibly accept save they go to pieces completely. Its meaning for the religious situation of the present can therefore be only indirect. It was possible for strong mystical forces to enter the Occident by a roundabout way through Russian literature, art and philosophy. It was possible, furthermore, for this effect to be increased through the presence of numerous, intellectually eminent representatives of Russian orthodoxy in the western nations and through the strong impression which its religious directness and solidity made upon the confused, disintegrated temper of the West. The question whether the Russian church, as a result of the deep catastrophes of the Russian spirit, will be able to take new and significant directions of development is wholly obscure for us. At present it cannot be regarded as an essential element in the religious situation of the West.

II. *Judaism.* Before we proceed to the consideration of the Protestant churches, it will be in order to pay attention to Judaism as a religious phenomenon. Judaism, like Protestantism in this respect, is in much closer contact with the spirit of capitalist society than is Catholicism, Roman or Greek. The close connection between religion and morality, the high evaluation of personality, the devaluation of the sacramental sphere, the secularization of nature, the exaltation of the law, religiously inspired intraworldly activity—all this is present in Judaism as in Protestantism and in capitalist society. It is common to all three not only because they are related types but also as a result of the historical influence of Judaism on the rise of capitalist society. It is not strange therefore that certain groups in humanistic, cultured Judaism readily and easily abandoned their religious heritage and transferred their loyalty to capitalist society. Yet the spirit of ancient prophecy continues to be effective even in religiously liberal circles.

For that reason it was possible for Jews such as Marx, Lassalle, Adler, Landauer and, in part, the leaders of the Russian revolution, to give expression to this spirit in their conflict with capitalistic society and to proclaim it in truly prophetic manner as in the Communist Manifesto. But because the religious heritage had been lost the after-effects of the activity of these men could not escape the fate of becoming subject to the spirit of bourgeois society.

The situation in orthodox Judaism is different. It is bound to tradition and contains valuable religious forces. But it carries them beneath an armor of Jewish ritualism. Therefore it is not of direct significance for the religious situation of the present. Eastern Judaism particularly is a reservoir of genuine and powerful religious tradition but a reservoir which cannot be directly tapped by the capitalist West.

A peculiar mixture of national and religious motives is evident in the Zionist movement. It is the expression of the longing for a national, religious center by a Judaism which though scattered among all the nations yet is religiously united. The nationalism which is stirring in this movement is not typical Western nationalism but a return to the original unity of religious prophecy and national existence. Opposition to the movement within Judaism itself is based on the danger which would attend the realization of the Zionist ideal. The peril is that the Jews scattered throughout the world would become foreigners everywhere, that a secular Jewish na-

eemed to be indissoluble. Throne
re brought into such close proxim-
only rôle left to the latter was the
vant. Under the circumstances the
f the hierarchical structure and the
of the absolute transcendence of
enged through the reduction of re-
ubordinate, this-worldly thing. It
ate in order that it might exist and
it was used and ruled by the state.
ediate present the situation is such
eran church stands in inner antag-
state which grew out of the demo-
ion, that it finds its main support
vative, nationalist groups and, in
not inconsiderable reënforcements
ups. In theory it rejects every po-
e. Practically it is orientated by its
rd a conservative, monarchical,
eaucratic, national and military
f this there is a large measure of
alist temper and it is intelligible
amental attitude of large groups
rians, peasants and laborers finds
pression in the Lutheran church.
nt church in Lutheran regions
e bourgeois only at the moment
l Liberalism began its triumphant
iumph was achieved in part with

tionalism might develop and that the universal,
messianic, world-uniting mission of Judaism
would suffer. Martin Buber represents a mysti-
cally profound Zionism. He envisions a mystical
ideal which the Jews are to realize and which is
to become a powerful symbol and emanative
force for the rest of the world. Buber's presentations of Jewish mysticism, which have literary as
well as other values, belong to the whole mystical movement against the spirit of capitalist
society. But this Jewish mysticism is always connected with the prophetic element of hope of
the consummation.

In many ways therefore there is evidence that
in Judaism also there is reaction—not without
backslidings—against the spirit of capitalist society. But the revolt encounters particular difficulties because of the close interrelation of large
circles of Jews with the capitalist system and its
exclusively commercial type of life.

III. *Protestantism.* (a) Protestantism and
Culture. Protestantism stands at the very center
of the problem of church and capitalist society.
Its history has proceeded in very close connection with the history of the capitalist spirit. Indeed, the popular exaggeration of Max Weber's
thesis about the significance of Calvinism for
the rise of the capitalist spirit often makes it appear as though Protestantism itself were noth-

ing but the capitalist spirit. On the contrary it may be asserted that original Protestantism was the sharpest protest it is possible to think of against the spirit of self-sufficient finitude, in its ecclesiastical and hierarchical as well as in its humanistic and rationalistic form. Luther raised his protest against both of these with dynamic, prophetic force in the name of that which is absolutely beyond, of the divine reality which prevails over all human activity. This protest was and remains alive, whether continued by orthodox Protestantism or by Protestant pietism. The peril of Protestantism lay in the fact that it was a protest and that it did not achieve an adequate realization. No church can be founded on a protest, yet Protestantism became a church. Consequently it needed to adopt positive elements out of tradition, but in such a way that they would not take the edge off the force of the protest; therefore it limited them and crowded them into the background to the point of neglect. As a result the protest lost its ultimate meaning and became a doctrine alongside of other doctrines. The inner dilemma of Protestantism lies in this, that it must protest against every religious or cultural realization which seeks to be intrinsically valid, but that it needs such realization if it is to be able to make its protest in any meaningful way.

All the separa
the present situ
tradition whicl
greatness and it
prophetic attac
archy broke do
ligiously finite
ness, was set as
arose as to wha
question remai
hood of pure d
self-esteem con
hood, arose wit
development w
maintain itself
ple of the gener
dition the prea
power of the C
that the vacant
powers, in Lutl
ism by society.

The relation
two secular po
fact. Lutheran
pendent on the
partment of ad
of antagonizing
with an absolu
ited monarchy

tive forces s
and altar we
ity that the
rôle of a ser
destruction c
proclamation
God were av
ligion to a
needed the s
consequently
In the imm
that the Lutl
onism to the
cratic revolu
in the conse
turn, recruits
for these gro
litical allianc
history towa
agrarian, bu
ideal. In all
the pre-capit
that the fund
of great agra
its proper ex
The Protesta
really becam
when nationa
march. The t

the aid of liberal Protestant theologians who, under the protection of the nation's enforcement of peace within the church, arrived at positions of influence and proclaimed Protestantism as a religion of national culture in which a self-sufficient finitude was religiously consecrated but was not invaded and questioned by the eternal. Nationalist suggestions and the hate of democracy and socialism are still too strong for Lutheran Protestantism as a whole to become aware of its apostasy. But at least the pagan extremes of the nationalist movement receive only limited applause within Protestantism and in an official proclamation the German Protestant churches have indicated their resolution to reject the extreme capitalistic principle.

The real difficulty which Lutheran Protestantism faces appears most clearly in those movements within it which are seeking for a solution of the social problem: the Church and Social Problems movement, the Evangelical Social movement, and Religious Socialism. The first of these represents an attempt to win the workers to a conservative Christian philosophy and attitude toward life. The attempt has failed on both sides. A truly earnest social passion on the part of the ruling powers, even on the part of the conservative party, was not to be thought of after the victory of the philosophy of national liberalism. On the other hand labor as a whole was absolutely incapable of adopting the conservative Protestant attitude which had been developed under entirely different social conditions than now prevail. The effectiveness of this movement at present is therefore inconsiderable and it was logical that the Christian Social party should have been taken up into the German National party. The Evangelical Social Congress is working more in the sphere of theory and from the viewpoint of liberal Protestantism. It has made many valuable scientific contributions but it is suffering, even from the point of view of science, from the fact that it does not subject Protestantism itself and capitalist society as a whole to fundamental criticism. It lacks the power of a hope for the future, of the consciousness of a real turn in time which will put all things in question. Consequently it is working not only too much in the realm of theory—which does no harm if the theory be good—but also without enthusiasm. It is too deeply immersed in the spirit of capitalist society to be able to go beyond it.

But the religious social movement also—more accurately Religious Socialism—is saddled with the burden of the fundamental problem of Protestantism. After its origins in the prophetic spirit of the Blumhardts it was brought into close relationship with socialism and pacifism by Ragaz in Switzerland, was referred by Kutter and in radical fashion by Barth and his school to its religious source, and finally robbed of any relation to socialism or to concrete social movements. It became in this instance a theoretical tendency in which the Protestant theme of the pure transcendence of God is expressed with great emphasis. But the question about realization, the question about the social environment which is necessary before such a proclamation can even be heard, the question as to the ability of our time to understand the proclamation—that is to say, all questions about the religious situation of our time as a concrete, unique reality are rejected by this tendency. In practice this naturally means the support of that which *is*, in our case the support of the spirit of a time controlled and formed by capitalist society.

The League of Religious Socialists has an ecclesiastical political character. It seeks to reconcile socialism and the Protestant church without radically changing either. But this intention must probably be accounted impractical in view of the present structure of both these entities.

The group whose organ is the journal *Blätter für Religiösen Sozialismus* has not established a confessional test but the Protestant spirit is strong enough in it to make the question about the relationship of divine transcendence to socialist realization in time of decisive importance. Whether the answer to this question will be such that it will have significance within Protestantism cannot be predicted. At all events all of these movements show the difficulty which exists for Protestantism when it attempts to offer practical opposition to the spirit of capitalist society.

This becomes even more apparent in the case of Calvinism. The position which was occupied in Lutheranism by the state at first and which now seems to be in danger of being occupied by the German National party was occupied in Calvinism by society since early times. In the conflict of Calvinism with princely authorities it was victorious in almost every instance. Often it was represented by emigrant communities. In neither case was it possible for the state to take the place of the old hierarchy. Hence the churches needed to create and administer their own constitution out of their own resources. The principle of voluntary membership and the democratic structure brought this type of Protestantism into close relation to the sectarian type and made the union of the two possible. The soil was prepared for the individualism of capitalist society, for the emasculation of the state, for the fundamental significance of the individual. The isolated individual is originally and in principle the religious individual; gradually he became more and more the type of individual who corresponds to the concept of democratic, capitalist society. The spirit of the religious community is impregnated with the spirit of capitalist society. On the other hand the latter receives constant reënforcement from the spirit of the Calvinist church. And therein lies its power. For this fact prevents its relapse into the open brutality of a demonic naturalism. Hence the faith is awakened in large sections of the church that capitalist humanism is the realization of the Christian ideal. A humanization of Christianity takes place which is always at the same time a Christianization of humanism. It is evident that on this soil a revolt against the spirit of capitalism is almost impossible. Despite the unprecedented and extreme development of the capitalistic system in the Anglo-American world capitalism has not yet revealed its true features and its demonic character to the consciousness of those nations. Even the socialism of these countries is more of an economic attack carried on by the laboring class for the sake of gaining a larger participation in the advantages of the system than an attack on the system itself. And the older manifestations of

religious socialism rest on the Calvinist principle of the church and on the demand that a
large part of one's economic gain be devoted to
the church and the poor. In this movement also
no fundamental opposition to the system itself
can be discovered. Accordingly there is no sign
of a consciousness of the crisis of the time and
of capitalist society.[1] An activist and tremen-
dously effective optimism instinctively identified
the Kingdom of God with a thoroughly human-
ized, pacifist, Christianized bourgeois humanity.
This does not mean that the problems which
have arisen in Europe are not important for
America. They are present in the nature of the
case and must appear in all their sharpness
sooner or later. At all events, for the present
the close relation between Calvinist Protestantism and capitalist society is an historic fact, the
significance of which for the contemporary religious situation cannot be overestimated.

The attitude of both Lutheranism and Calvinism toward the various social problems is extremely conservative and legal in the religious

[1] When the German edition of this book was published in
1926 Tillich's comment on the situation in England and
America was more applicable. Even so, native observers of
earlier events and movements in these countries will need
to disagree with his interpretation at some points, though
they may agree with the description as a whole.—*Translator.*

sense. The relationship of the sexes is governed by the unconditional demand for exclusive monogamy. This is even truer of the Calvinist than of the Lutheran form of Protestantism. But the latter also has closed its mind almost completely to the problems which are present in this sphere. The churches do not see that through their shyness they support the hypocrisy of bourgeois conventionality on the one hand and, on the other, exclude themselves from the great, continent-wide discussion of the sex-relationship. Hence they do not come to grips with the task of offering a solution which will point to the transcendent sphere but which will not be purely legal and conventional. In this case also it becomes apparent how difficult is the situation into which they have been forced by their destruction of the sacramental character of marriage on the one hand and of voluntary celibacy on the other. They have no point of departure from which they can make the attempt to emancipate themselves from their union with bourgeois convention.

It has been pointed out above that the youth movement within the Protestant churches was least able of all to find a soil friendly to its development. Its antithesis to the spirit of capitalist society necessarily brought it into antithesis to the characteristic Protestant attitude in view of the deep roots of that spirit in Protestantism as well as in Judaism.

Because Protestantism has no definite ideal of culture, education in its sphere of influence can result only in a dualism of religious faith and humanistic idealism in which the former is ultimately forced aside. The situation in our whole higher educational system speaks eloquently of this fact. It is well known how destructive of religion is the influence exercised by a religious instruction which is carried on in connection with the other subjects of the curriculum. It is one of the most important causes of the abandonment of the Protestant church by the larger part of the educated world.

The roots of all these problems of Protestantism lie in the difficulty of the Protestant ethics. The destruction of the Catholic ideal of saintliness and the emphasis on the transcendence of God, which makes every religious realization questionable, leave a vacuum which is occupied by the humanistic ideal, the emotional motive of which is the appeal to obedience to law and the actual character of which is conformity to bourgeois convention. At scarcely any point have the Protestant churches made a serious attempt to surmount this difficulty. On the contrary the extreme tendency in Protestant theology is inclined to banish ethics entirely out of the theological system; only the religious socialist and the religious nationalist movements are seeking new paths in this region, partly in connection with the theology of German idealism and romanticism and with recourse to the theologians of culture such as Schleiermacher and Richard Rothe. It is very doubtful whether these attempts will have any success within the Protestant churches and the danger is great that even should they succeed to a certain extent they will adjust themselves again to the spirit of capitalist society. For the problem is rooted very deeply in the whole Protestant attitude.

In the theoretic sphere not even an earnest attempt has been made to attain to a Protestant ideal of culture. Protestantism avoids every direct and indirect influence upon art without noticing that art is constantly exercising influences which run counter to the Protestant conception of the transcendence of God and the secular character of nature and which are leading the mind away from bourgeois Protestantism. There really is no relationship of Protestantism to painting and sculpture. A smooth, idealized realism in the spirit of bourgeois convention is almost exclusively dominant. The new forms created or discovered by expressionism meet violent opposition, particularly on the part of the church. A happier situation prevails in literature although in this case also the really great artists have scarcely been recognized by the Protestant church. Happiest of all is the situation in music, where the old Protestant tradition has not wholly ceased and where Bach and the Protestant choral reveal the superiority of the heroic old Protestant spirit over capitalist society.

In science and philosophy the wearisome ineffective battle waged by the church in self-defense came to an end through the radical separation of the territories of faith and of knowledge and through the unconditional surrender of the field of battle to autonomous science. One postulated the existence of a pagan brain beside a Christian heart and rested content. The solution had the value of putting an end to all attempts to deduce proofs of the eternal from the finite and its forms. It made impossible the use of gaps in scientific knowledge for the sake of introducing God as a gap-filler in the scientific description of the world. It forced the recognition that the eternal appears at a deeper level than the level of rational thought. But, on the other hand, the definition of this level as feeling and the inability of bringing it into relationship to the scientific view of reality led to the separation of the whole sphere of truth from religion. Religion left it alone to work out its finite realization. And religion itself was dealt with as a matter of subjective moods which could make no claims to understand or reform the world. Thus the typically impressionistic, bourgeois attitude entered into religion: upon the one side rational science, a system of self-sufficient forms, on the other side subjective feeling, which did not have the power to break through the finite.

Orthodoxy fought against this secularization constantly and with emphasis. It taught that there were invasions of the system of finite forms—miracles, inspiration, creation, beginning and end. Yet it regarded these concepts not as religious ideas but as scientific and theoretical concepts which were used not so much to break through as to break up the system of finite forms. The result was that it entered into a fruitless opposition and was gradually forced to adopt the strategy of that constantly retreating apologetics, surrendering position after position, to which we referred above. When orthodoxy conceived its ideas in theoretical, scientific fashion it had accepted so much of the bourgeois spirit that it could not escape defeat.

The change which took place in this situation is connected with the entrance of mystical and intuitive elements into Protestant theology. Rudolf Otto's book on *Religion and Naturalism* was an attempt to go beyond the dilemma of the situation, to grasp the unique, independent character of religious concepts and to free apologetics of its intolerable burden. One must rejoice over the fact that since that time the situation with regard particularly to the natural sciences has been cleared up to a great extent even within the churches. History still creates difficulties. For the religious view there is in history a super-temporal element, which cannot be reduced to historical terms but which must not be placed alongside of secular history as something which has a separate history. The problem gave rise to the same antithesis as did the problem of nature. On the one side there was the rationalized, orthodox theory that a sacred history of miraculous sort parallels secular history—a theory which breaks up the unity of historical knowledge. On the other side there was the rational, liberal theory that sacred history is nothing but a part of general history—a theory which leaves the self-sufficient finitude of the historical untouched and unbroken. The struggle for a new metaphysics of history has led us somewhat beyond these alternatives.

So theology is laboring to gain a right relationship to the scientific sphere and to seize upon the approaches made to it from the side of science. The development is still in its beginnings. It can arrive at its goal only when the situation in the religious, theological sphere, in the narrow sense, has come to sufficient maturity.

(b) Religious Life in Protestantism. From an early time onward two tendencies have been evident in the religious life of Protestantism, the ecclesiastical dogmatic tendency and the pietistic. Both tendencies had their sources in Luther's attitude and both have developed in Protestantism down to the present day. At the end of the seventeenth century they stood in sharp contrast to each other as Orthodoxy and Pietism; in the eighteenth century rationalism was added as a third element. At present actual Protestant religion is influenced by all three forms. There is the ecclesiastical, positive tendency which must be described as a greatly softened orthodoxy; the antithesis to this tendency is the ecclesiastical liberal movement, which may be defined as a moderate Illuminism; the pietist tendency with its fellowships stands in contrast to both of the former movements but at the same time it has peculiar positive relations to both. The liberal tendency approaches closely to, or is almost absorbed by, the temper of capitalist society. It attempts to make religion a part of the system of finite forms, either as their crown or their unity. It represents itself to be a cultural Protestantism which is quite aware of morality but little aware of the shaking of culture by the eternal. It has relatively little significance for the religious life. Its sermons are not wanted for they contain nothing that points beyond the self-sufficient finite world. Autonomous culture does not require the religious change of names which liberal Protestantism wants to bestow upon it. It tolerates this liberalism, defends it even, but does not really respect it because it does not have the power to oppose the culture. The excellence of liberal Protestantism lies in the scientific sphere, in theology insofar as theology must be the science of religion. But even in systematic theology the same limitations become apparent which are present in the practical religious attitude. The spirit of self-sufficient finitude is not transcended by liberalism either theoretically or practically.

The positive tendency in contrast to liberalism has a great advantage. It possesses the old, pre-capitalist tradition; it is sharply negative towards civilization and this-worldliness; it is always willing to allow the unity of the autonomous spirit to come to grief in every sphere. Therefore its effectiveness continues to be great and its sermons are still listened to. It controls the church almost completely. At the same time it is not stiff and petrified but elastic, particularly in its reception of modern science. One may even say that its antithesis to liberal theology has been canceled in the whole field of scientific research in religion even where this research deals with the Bible and the church. Yet even this positive tendency has shown no evidence of ability to conquer the capitalist spirit. In part it has rejected the latter by relying on methods which were quite as irreligious and as rationalistic as those which were rejected; in part it has made compromises which have robbed it of its deepest strength without being adequate to the justifiable claims of autonomous science. Because of this half and half character it is weaker than is the liberal tendency. Its strength lies in the fact that it encourages preaching to tap the springs of the pre-capitalist, prophetic and priestly spirit in religion.

Pietistic religion develops its practice and theory without making the compromises of orthodoxy. It is an attempt to realize Protestantism not only in ecclesiastical and dogmatic but in vital forms. It is connected by many lines with Catholic Jesus-mysticism which, however, it has bent in a strongly personalistic and ethical direction. It is a constant source of religious power for Protestantism. Again and again it has given birth to revolts against the spirit of capitalist society. On the one hand its transcendence of all this-worldliness and bondage to civilization, on the other hand its strong interest in fellowship, stands in violent antithesis to bourgeois this-worldliness and to spiritual individualism. In addition, pietism has conserved the religious tradition of the past on the practical religious side to a much greater extent than orthodoxy has done. Yet in pietism also the total situation of our time becomes evident. First of all for pietism as for Protestantism in general the personal character of religion is of decisive importance. Therein the individualism of capitalist society is represented. Furthermore, pietism in common with the rest of Protestantism lacks a permanent, priestly actualization of religion. It is quite logical therefore that the old pietism should have prepared the way to a large extent for the Illumination and that contemporary pietism should not have the power to conquer the spirit of capitalist society. On the contrary, it has aided this spirit in many ways. Upon the one hand it took over from orthodoxy that fruitless dogmatic rigidity which orthodoxy itself has softened so that at this point a complete change of front occurred; on the other hand in most recent times it has diverged into the camp of the nationalists in a most peculiar and inexplicable fashion and in contradiction to its own spirit.

With all of this it combines great activity in church politics in an extremely orthodox direction. These processes in which the contraction and secularization of pietism become evident at the same time, indicate clearly how tremendous is the power which the spirit of the present exercises even upon movements which are opposed to it.

Such is the character of the three main tendencies in the Protestant church. None of them leads us beyond the present situation. They vacillate between protest against and compromise with the spirit of capitalist society. Other movements have not as yet gone beyond the stage of theological consideration. Movements which are of importance for religious life and which have prospects of future development are not to be found at the present time in the Protestant church. Even religious socialism, whether represented by the Neuwerk group or the Berlin circle or by the church-political League of Religious Socialists, cannot make the claim to such significance. What Protestantism possesses in the way of significant movements is to be found in the theological sphere—which is quite characteristic of Protestantism.

This judgment denies the decisive importance of two factors which are receiving a great deal of attention. The first of these is the increase of the influence of the church, the second is the high church movement. It is not strange that the evangelical church should also profit by the general turn toward religion. But to account for the increase of the influence of the church other factors besides this one must be taken into consideration. The alliance of the church with the conservative nationalist attitude has greatly strengthened its reputation in all circles which represent the latter tendency. But the question whether this political, ecclesiastical gain has not been purchased at the cost of great religious loss must be raised emphatically. A further reason for the increase of ecclesiastical influence even upon labor is that many parents, including socialist parents and particularly mothers, feel that education without religion and a philosophy of life lacks content. Since socialism stands for the secularized school—a position which is logical from the capitalist but doubtful from the socialist point of view—it contributes indirectly to the strengthening of evangelical Parents' Leagues and so to the strengthening of the evangelical church in general. Yet no essential significance for our religious situation can be ascribed to the contemporary increase of the power of the church. These things are all too superficial for that.

The high church movement, that is the attempt to increase the psychological effectiveness of the evangelical churches through reforms of worship and constitution, is more important. These efforts evidently start with the problem of actualizing the Protestant principle which is the fundamental Protestant problem and they therefore deserve attention. Naturally they tend toward Catholic forms of life, a fact which makes them a part of the general Catholicizing tendency of the time and which has led to divisions within the movement itself. On the principle of the movement the following judgment may be passed—the hierarchy and ritual of Catholicism rest upon the Catholic sacraments and their unassailable objectivity. But this is just what has been destroyed by Protestantism. Every attempt at a new Catholic actualization of the ideas of priesthood or ritual must either violate the Protestant principle or remain a matter of pedagogic compromises. Protestantism rests upon preaching, on the proclamation of a transcendent God who is above all attempts at human actualization. This God has no sacraments which can be divorced from the prophetic message and therefore no priesthood and no genuine cult. Yet even preaching when it is not inspired prophecy presupposes a priestly and ritual attitude. Essentially it is the negation of priesthood and ritual yet at the same time it becomes a new basis for both. At this point again the fundamental problem of Protestantism appears, a problem which high-church movements will not solve at all events. Therefore a decisive significance for our present religious situation can be ascribed to this tendency as little as to the increased power of the church. For that matter it is developing within very modest limits, both in theory and in influence.

The rejection of the spirit of capitalist society and the search for a new fulfillment of the Christian idea are more clearly evident in Protestant theology than in the movements just mentioned. Liberalism was and, to a certain extent, remains dominant in theology. Positive theology was unable to offer anything even remotely equal in value to the brilliant achievements of liberal scholarship in the field of history. As a result of the destruction of the specious historical foundations of the orthodox system—particularly through the critical study of the gospels and the interpretation of primitive Christianity from the point of view of history of religion—the situation of positive theology, even in dogmatics, became constantly more difficult. Its strength lay in its content, its weakness in its scientific form. It lost ground steadily and even in the thoughtful form of modern-positive theology it was unable to regain anything of essential importance.

The most significant change came from other quarters. First of all it occurred in liberal theology itself. The historical method logically led to the comprehensive, penetrating study of the whole history of religion. Psychology of religion and disinterested evaluation of religious phenomena rendered important aid. The world of religious life disclosed its great originality and universality. The rationalistic and moralistic interpretaton of religion which had prevailed in liberal theology broke down. The ecstatic, form-destroying character of religion with its divine and demonic aspects was recognized. Working on these bases Rudolf Otto offered a splendidly developed phenomenology of religion in his book on *The Idea of the Holy*. From this point lines of relationship to idealistic and romantic theology could be traced. On all sides theology broke through the Kantian walls which surrounded it. The eternal was apprehended as the ground of meaning and the abyss of reality and only in the second place as a demand and as law. It was possible to speak again of a fundamental, divine revelation which lies at a deeper level than every concrete revelation.

Therewith the alternative between liberalism

and orthodoxy was surmounted. The religious ideas and religious forms of life are neither to be reduced after the fashion of liberalism to parts of the system of finite forms nor are they to be apprehended in orthodox fashion as destructive of that system. They are concepts of transcendence beyond the form, not of the breaking of forms. Neither capitalist autonomy nor ecclesiastical heteronomy—for both belong together—but theonomy, the free devotion of finite forms to the eternal, is the goal. No systematic elaboration of these ideas has as yet been made. It would entail a thoroughgoing transformation of tradition and of the liberal forms into which they were analyzed, but it would need to carry on a constant battle against both sides; yet it would also be able to aid the religious symbols to regain the expressive force which will allow a whole period to find its eternal meaning in them.

Alongside of this tendency which is greatly under the influence of the whole mystical movement of our times, there is another tendency which consciously and emphatically seeks to return to Luther. Karl Holl's book on Luther is the strongest expression of this theology. Its influence is rather considerable, particularly on the young theologians. They are actually speaking of a Luther-Renaissance. In this movement also there is the desire to go beyond the antithesis of orthodox and liberal and to open up again the fountains of prophetic religion. And it also has lines of relationship to idealism and romanticism. But no decisive importance for the total movement of our times can be conceded to this movement, for it knows nothing of an explicit denial of the spirit of capitalist society and in consequence it appears in its practical effects and in part in its theoretical expressions also to strengthen that spirit. A Luther-Renaissance on the basis of the present religious situation, regarded as a whole, is an impossibility.

This is also true of the third theological tendency, the dialectical or, as it is now also called, the Neo-Reformed theology. It grew out of religious socialism and is extremely powerful. Its fundamental document is Karl Barth's *Commentary on the Epistle to the Romans,* a book of truly prophetic power and penetration. This theology lets the judgment of the unconditionedly transcendent God fall upon every attempt of culture or religion to claim value before him. In its conception the only relation which the world has to God is that the world stands in the divine negation, in the crisis, in the shaking of time by eternity. In consequence mysticism and romanticism, idealism and the religious ideal of civilization are sharply rejected. Civilization may go on its own independent way but it must be subjected as a whole to the judgment. The system of finite forms is to remain as it is, but must be broken through as a whole. There can be no doubt that this theology is of the highest importance for the religious situation of the present. But it is also clear that it can turn into an actual reënforcement of the spirit of capitalist society and of its orthodox correlate as soon as the prophetic disturbance of our days has ceased—as it must cease—and as soon as self-sufficient finitude stands before us once more unassailed and unchanged.

The present situation in theology can be surmounted only by way of a union of the priestly spirit of the first and the prophetic spirit of the third of the above-mentioned movements. Such a union we can again designate as belief-ful realism. At all events abundant and strong life is moving in the Protestant theology of our time. There is apparent in it the will to break through futile antitheses within the bourgeois situation. The decisive turn if it is to take place anywhere in Protestantism may be expected in theology.

We have arrived at the end of our study. It has shown us in every sphere from the natural sciences to ritual and dogma the turning away from the spirit of self-sufficient finitude, from the spirit of capitalist society. It has also shown us the difficulties, aberrations and reactions of this movement and has designated belief-ful realism as the attitude which is proper to our present situation. One thing however must be remembered in connection with all of these observations: they can have meaning only for those who are themselves engaged in the movement and for them they are not only meaningful but also full of responsibility. Such men are not permitted to stand aloof as non-participating observers, but it is demanded of them that they think and speak about the religious situation of the present with unconditioned, active responsibility.